Building Overseas

Butterworth Architecture Management Guide

Francis Baden-Powell
RMJM

Butterworth Architecture
An imprint of Butterworth-Heinemann Ltd
Linacre House, Jordan Hill, Oxford OX2 8DP

 PART OF REED INTERNATIONAL BOOKS

OXFORD   LONDON   BOSTON
MUNICH   NEW DELHI   SINGAPORE   SYDNEY
TOKYO   TORONTO   WELLINGTON

First published 1993

British Library Cataloguing in Publication Data
Baden-Powell, Francis
  Building Overseas
  I. Title
  720.68

ISBN 0 7506 0331 3

Library of Congress Cataloguing in Publication Data
Baden-Powell, Francis.
  Building overseas/Francis Baden-Powell.
  p. cm.
  Includes bibliographical references and index.
  ISBN 0 7506 0331 3
  1. Architectural practice, International.   I. Title.
  NA 1996.B29
  720'.68–dc20
                                                              92–21710
                                                              CIP
Printed in Great Britain by Redwood Press Ltd, Melksham, Wiltshire

Building Overseas

To the wives and children who stayed at home

Contents

Foreword

By His Royal Highness The Duke of Gloucester, GCVO, President, British Consultants Bureau

The engineers and architects of the nineteenth century not only pioneered new methods of building and of designing, they also pioneered the organization and working practices of their professions. The professions in this country have always valued their independence, not only from any government control but also from manufacturers or contractors. The obligation is only to the client who is paying for an unbiased opinion. This tradition is different from many other countries and it has given the British consultant an advantage over many other nationalities.

It is easy to prove this by the remarkable success that British consultants have had over many decades, and not only in those countries helped by multinational organizations such as development banks and those trying to build effective infrastructures in Third World countries. This has occurred at a time when most countries actively promote the growing skills of their own professionals – a process in which British consultants have often involved themselves at a personal level, creating a network of contacts that have proved invaluable.

As national boundaries continue to diminish in importance the traditional British consultant is likely to become even more relevant to solving the problems of other countries, even if his 'Britishness' is less relevant. It is not a matter of cultural imperialism, but simply that our traditions give us a more relevant 'international' outlook and this enables us to be flexible enough to solve many problems that more rigid systems tackle less effectively.

Working abroad involves more risks than staying at home, but this may bring compensations in achieving a greater effect on the quality of life of many millions of people, and a satisfaction in being able to benefit other people from the quality of our own experience.

Francis Baden-Powell is well experienced in foreign projects and I believe his book is timely, for it is my experience that there are many people around the world who welcome a British consultant and the tradition of integrity he brings with him. That this is a marketable commodity I have no doubt, but it must, of course, be accompanied by a competence to appreciate local factors that will affect the project. This book considers these factors and should provide an admirable guide and, I hope, an encouragement to many home-based professionals to take the plunge and thus extend their horizons in every sense.

Preface

By Francis Baden-Powell

The initiative for writing this book comes from the article which I wrote in 1988 on International Practice for the *Wilkes Encyclopedia of Architecture*, which focused my mind on the differences between working as an architect in the UK and overseas. Having travelled abroad for fifteen years on a wide variety of jobs for RMJM I felt that it would be useful to distil this experience, and that of my colleagues in RMJM, for a wider readership.

When we first worked overseas in the 1960s British architects had a strong competitive edge in developing countries in the Commonwealth and in some oil-rich countries. Since then "Commonwealth preference" has disappeared, and new markets (as, for example, in the EC) have opened up. The market should thus be regarded as truly world-wide, where British architects are in competition with architects from the rest of the world to make the most of our innate skills and experience.

I assume generally that the reader will represent a firm of architects wishing to work overseas, with the exception of Chapter 13, which is addressed to an individual architect wishing to work overseas for a firm of architects (whether British or foreign) or for a development agency.

Structure of this book

This book follows the logic of seeking, winning and carrying out a single project overseas, with a sideways look at the implications of having a local office (whether it be for a branch of your UK firm, a separate local firm or a joint venture) which carries out work on more than one project. It is written on a worst-case principle, using experience in developing and oil-rich countries as examples. Some aspects may not be so relevant to work in developed countries, but should be useful in providing a checklist to ensure that nothing is missed.

I do not attempt here to repeat any of the procedures which you follow for acquiring and designing projects and getting them built in the UK. You will, of course, largely carry out these procedures on overseas projects too. I do, however, try to identify what we in RMJM have found to be different about building overseas, or additional to what you would normally do in the UK. It is these aspects which you will need to understand, and to take account of, if your work overseas is to be successful and profitable.

Some Definitions

People

In this book I have used "he" "him" "his" when referring to individuals, for brevity. However, in every case these imply "he or she", "him or her" "his or hers" etc., although in some countries (such as Saudi Arabia) it is difficult (if not impossible) to envisage your local representative being a woman. References to "we" or "our" are to the combined experience of members of RMJM.

Currency

For simplicity throughout the book I have adopted the following symbols:

£ for UK pounds sterling
$ for US dollars

Other currencies are spelt out in full.

Acronyms

For brevity I have used a number of acronyms in common use among consultants working overseas. For readers unfamiliar with them I have included a glossary in Appendix C.

Bibliography

Apart from specific references listed numerically for the book as a whole, I have included in Appendix E a number of general references which provide useful background reading on this subject.

Acknowledgements

I would particularly like to record my thanks to my colleagues in RMJM for contributing their experience both in the individual case studies and on other projects, and on administrative aspects: to David Nelson of Sir Norman Foster & Partners and to Armando Figuereido of Norman & Dawbarn for the case studies of work in Japan and Tanzania which so usefully complement RMJM's experience; to Peter MacGregor, ex-Director of EGCI, for access to checklists which his member firms use for appraisals of overseas markets; to Max Carruthers, Managing Director of Alfred Blackmore & Co Ltd, for advice on Professional Indemnity Insurance overseas; to the BCB for its guidance notes which provide the basis for Section 11.5 on ECGD; to Alan Smith of Bickerdike Allen and Partners, and to Clifford Lansley for progress reports on EC Directives; to my wife Cherry for proof-reading and suggesting how to make the text easier to read; and to Jennie Kaylor for skilfully and patiently processing and reprocessing the manuscript.

FB-P

Introduction

By Sir Andrew Derbyshire, President, RMJM

Our late-lamented client and friend, His Excellency Soliman Abdel Hai, had extensive experience in employing expatriate consultants for reconstruction work in Egypt after the outbreak of peace in 1973. He was fond of quoting a story about two frogs and an owl. It went like this:

> Two frogs were suffering acutely from cold and were advised to engage a consultant to deal with the problem. The owl, being very wise, had built up a great consulting reputation. The frogs explained the problem to him and he agreed to study it and to present them with a report on payment of a suitable fee. In due course his report arrived, together with the account for his services; the one recommendation was that the frogs should grow feathers. The frogs thanked him for his valuable advice, paid his fee and started to try to grow feathers. Some time later they went back to the owl and complained that his advice was not practical. The owl replied 'I am a consultant whom you asked to prepare a recommendation, which I have now done. How you implement it is your affair.'

This tells us a lot about the fears of many of our overseas clients – that all they will get out of employing us is unusable advice and unbuildable designs.

This is not altogether the architect's fault. People in the countries of the developing world are often too proud to admit their poverty and expect Western advisers to provide them with Western solutions however inappropriate they may be. Thus we see magnificent air-conditioned offices with occupants sweltering during one of the regular power failures and gleaming new airports and high-rise luxury flats surrounded by squatter camps.

But is it our responsibility to try to impose our moral standards on politicians who belong to a different culture and embrace a religious belief in which we cannot share? This looks dangerously like intellectual colonialism and would be rightly resented. What we have to do instead is to expose the facts, offer options for choice, and leave our clients to make the final decision. And the options must all be based on a real understanding of the realities of the place in human and emotional terms, as well as an honest acknowledgement of the physical and financial constraints. We have found that the mutual respect generated by this approach joins with our reputation for integrity to make British consultants welcome all over the world, and specially in our ex-colonies.

What are the practical implications of this policy of designing for implementation? Again to quote Soliman Abdel Hai:

> It is very important that the consultant works within the country he is serving and develops an understanding of the real nature of the problems with which he is dealing. He needs to develop a certain 'sense of the country' and be willing to spend time with local officials to learn of their approaches to specific development problems and of the bureaucratic framework. . . . Working in the country should not be restrained to an air-conditioned office and car, a luxury flat in the diplomatic quarter and field trips to the project area. Study tours to diverse parts of the nation, relating to various income groups, and travel in public conveyances are 'musts'. . . . Consultants must attempt to 'work themselves out of a job' even though they may be convinced that local professionals may still need foreign specialist advice . . . [and] . . . must live with the project and its environment, make maximum use of local experience and benefit from existing building technology and procedures, however simple they may be.

It is axiomatic that it is essential always to identify a local English-speaking associate who will work as a member of the team and be paid the appropriate rate for his services. Such people are hard to find but once discovered often become friends for life.

This all sounds like hard and uncomfortable work, so why do we do it? There are three main reasons as far as RMJM is concerned. First of all, to fill in the troughs in our UK workload and keep our core professional team intact while maintaining our profitability. It is unusual for the whole world to be at the bottom of the economic cycle simultaneously and we believe that geographical diversity is essential for the long-term survival of a large multi-disciplinary practice. It is important, however, not to put all our eggs in one basket, and particularly not to concentrate on work overseas at the expense of the home market. Second, because we acknowledge a moral responsibility to do what we can to respond to the global problems of poverty, inadequate shelter, lack of social services and badly managed urban growth accelerating at a horrifying rate. Third, to make what contribution we can to the invisible earnings which do a great deal to reduce our adverse balance of trade.

We have been fortunate in the world-wide outlook bequeathed to us by one of our founding partners, the late Sir Robert Matthew, who was President of the IUA and the CAA, as well as being President of the RIBA. His travels, and those of other partners who followed him, led to a wide experience of work in developing countries, to the oil-rich countries of the Middle East, and then to the more highly developed countries of the Pacific Rim. The benefits of this experience are just as relevant in the emerging markets of Western and Eastern Europe, and in order to make the most of these markets RMJM has recently launched a European network of architectural practices, Designers International, of which we are the British member.

There are other less tangible benefits which have become apparent to us during the last 35 years. We learnt how to make competitive fee bids before it was *de rigueur* at home, keep project cash flow positive and collect fees when due in spite of labyrinthine local tax structures and financial rules. Working in a strange, sometimes hostile, environment is a great sorter out of people. Weaknesses are embarrassingly revealed for all to see, as well as gratifyingly unexpected strengths. Isolation in a strange land forces a collaborative frame of mind and bonds are established which continue for the life of a career. They say that travel broadens the mind; it also generates self-confidence in those who succeed, and teaches management skills in a way which no business school could emulate. It is conversely essential that those who are not succeeding are rescued and counselled without delay. Prolonged misery can cause lifelong damage. Building abroad also provides young designers with opportunities to do big things at high speed which they would be very lucky to do at home, especially during a recession. For those with the right frame of mind it is a deeply satisfying and enriching experience.

What we have learnt in this way about responding quickly to unexpected challenges and developing an efficient and creative organization structure has had a powerful impact on the whole RMJM business. It is no accident that we have given up partnership as unwieldy and now have a corporate structure based on a holding company sheltering a group of subsidiary profit centres. And no one should be surprised that most of the senior people in the company have worked abroad, often together – including, of course, the author of this book.

He has courageously attempted to distil this wealth of experience to produce a unique work. The case studies in particular bring the generalities to life in a way which, to my knowledge, has never been done before. For the sake of brevity and relevance these have been deliberately restricted to work which is either current or has been completed during the last ten years. RMJM projects necessarily predominate because the information and experience is readily to hand, but I am delighted that we have been able to include projects by two other British practices – Sir Norman Foster & Partners and Norman & Dawbarn – which widen the perspective by covering countries in which we have not worked.

Our hope is that for those who have not yet built abroad this book will be an encouragement to try, a guide to success and a map of some of the pitfalls to be avoided. For those already in the business we offer a checklist to compare with theirs, and an insight into what the competition is up to.

In case we have overdone the gypsy's warnings my last word is that building abroad can be extremely rewarding – so long as you understand the risks and take the necessary steps to reduce them to an affordable level. Good luck!

1
Working Abroad

This book is about the process of designing and contract administration of buildings outside the UK. It is not particularly about the end-product, the buildings themselves, but uses a number of case studies to illustrate aspects which are important in the process of designing them and getting them built.

With the current overmanning of the architectural profession and shortages of work in the UK it is likely that more and more firms will want to work overseas, and export the skills developed in this country during the building boom in the 1980s. Although in principle the process is much the same as in the UK, in practice it may be significantly different, and it is important to understand the differences before embarking on an overseas assignment for a client. Inevitably the differences are most acute when working in poorer developing countries, but the questions which reveal the differences can usefully be applied to all overseas work.

You and the members of your firm have probably grown up in the UK, gained your professional experience here, and are familiar with the ways in which projects get designed and built in this country. Overseas many aspects of design and management may be quite different in weight and importance, and professional practice may be materially different.

It is essential to have some understanding of the people of the country for whom you are designing, their culture, their political economy and their national objectives, and how they hope to achieve them. You need to understand the physical climate, which probably in the past has led to fascinating and characteristic solutions to the problems of shelter, and the state of development of their construction technology and building industry.

Architects work abroad for many different reasons. You may be invited because of the quality of your published work, or you may be trying to fill the troughs in workload in the UK. You may be seeking work for altruistic reasons: for example, to help solve some of the appalling problems of basic shelter, or of providing for health or educational needs in developing countries. Whatever your reason for working abroad, there will be radical differences from working at home. Much more time will be spent on people: choosing the right person to go overseas to head a local office or be resident on site, dealing with that person's needs and those of his family. Much more time will be spent on administration: on getting paid adequately, and in good time, being able to transfer fees back to contribute to running the practice at home, on timely completion and auditing of local accounts and payment of local taxes, and on dealing with a multitude of unexpected contingencies from civil unrest to devaluation of local currencies.

Working overseas should be regarded as a long-term investment, to which resources of people and money must be committed, but which, when managed creatively, can give great personal satisfaction as well as commercial success and achievement.

We have found working overseas enjoyable and rewarding, for the quality of service we have been able to give to overseas clients, for the opportunity to respond to some of the fundamental challenges facing the world today, for the chance to work in new climates and cultures, and for freedom from some of the irritating constraints we suffer at home.

1.1 Overseas Clients

Countries in which clients may be found fall broadly into three categories:

(a)   **Developed countries** (with industrial market economies)

high-income economies with a Gross National Product (GNP) per capita more than $6000 in 1989, mainly located in:
  Western Europe
  North America
  The Pacific Rim.

(b) **Oil-rich countries**, for which exports of petrol and gas predominate in the national economy, mainly located in:
  The Middle East
  Africa.

(c) **Developing countries**: middle- and low-income economies with a GNP per capita less than $6000 in 1989, mainly located in:
  Eastern Europe
  CIS (formerly the USSR)
  Asia
  Africa
  Central and South America.

The dividing lines vary depending on definitions adopted by organizations such as the World Bank and ODA, and the availability of statistics. See Figure 1 based on the World Bank's grouping of economies in its *World Development Report 1991*[1].

A better measure of developmental status might be a Physical Quality of Life Index based on socio-economic progress incorporating life expectancy and infant mortality (representing the sum of the effects of nutrition, public health, income and environment) and literacy rate (as a measure of well-being and an important skill in the developmental process). However, figures are not generally available for such an index, and so the cruder index of GNP per capita will have to do instead.

Most developed and some developing countries have well-established architectural professions capable of carrying out most work, and regulated or represented by bodies similar to ARCUK and the RIBA in the UK. There is thus likely to be strong competition from local firms and a requirement to set up local offices to conform to the host country's professional regulations. On the other hand, many oil-rich and developing countries have less well-established (or even non-existent) architectural professions so that opportunities for British architects are greater. The situation is changing rapidly, however, as local architects increase in expertise and become more numerous.

Projects in developing countries are very much dependent on

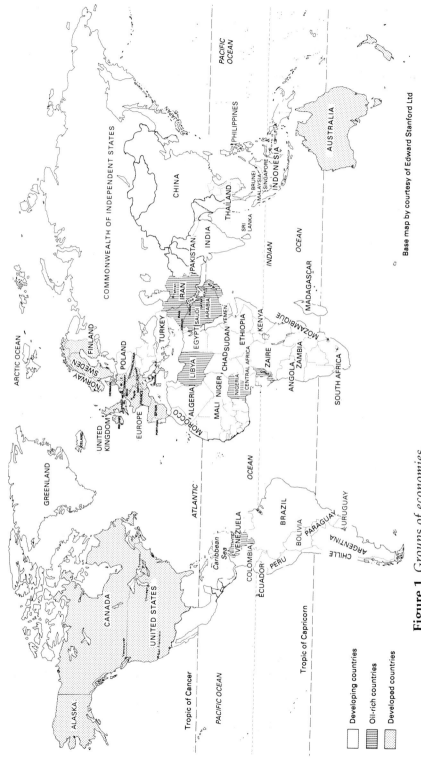

Figure 1 *Groups of economies.*

Base map by courtesy of Edward Stanford Ltd

Developing countries

Oil-rich countries

Developed countries

foreign funding. The major sources are the Multilateral Development Agencies (such as the World Bank, the European Development Fund, the Inter-American, Asian and African Development Banks, other United Nations Agencies, the Islamic Development Bank) and bilateral agencies (such as ODA, USAID, OECF). Projects tend to be related to planning, infrastructure, housing, health, education, tourism and leisure.

Opportunities for reconstruction exist after wars and natural disasters (as we experienced in Suez after the Arab–Israeli war and other firms in the Falklands and Armenia). Current examples are provided by Kuwait, Iran and Iraq.

Clients abroad parallel the whole range of those in the public and private sectors of the UK. They also include multinational corporations (such as banks, commercial and industrial conglomerates) and the UK government (including embassies and military installations).

As in the UK, there is a growth of package-deal or turnkey projects (which are often preferred by less experienced end-users) in which case the architect's immediate client is a contractor or equipment manufacturer and not the end-user, which can give rise to difficult questions of professional loyalty.

Projects on which expatriate architects are appointed are usually specialized (such as RMJM's management of a programme of schools in Nigeria for the World Bank), or buildings which are technically complex. These are illustrated by Case Studies 2 (Mbeya Hospital), 4 (Kota Kinabalu Airport), and 11 (Marine Research Laboratories, Aden).

There may seem to be a bewilderingly wide range of potential clients, but in Chapter 2, I suggest an approach to marketing your sevices which can provide a guide for newcomers to working overseas.

1.2 Executive or Advisory

An architect may work in an executive capacity overseas in the same way as in the UK, undertaking every stage in a project from briefing through design and production information to contract administration. Many of the case studies which are included as illustrations in this book are full executive projects of this kind.

However, with the wealth of local professional expertise in developed countries and the growth of indigenous architectural capability in other countries, British architects will more and more find themselves only partially in an executive role, and partially or wholly acting as consultants in an advisory capacity.

Case Study 3 (Jeddah Corniche) is an example of a project planned and designed by RMJM which was then used by the client to obtain tenders for detail-and-build contractors. Case Study 7 (Jeddah Historic Area) is an example of a project where we set the scene for a series of conservation projects, training counterparts in how to carry them out, and then acted as advisers to those counterparts when they in turn carried later projects through. Case Study 9 (CIMA, Colombo) is an example of an entirely advisory assignment to a client in appointing local consultants in Sri Lanka, and advising on every stage of the carrying through of the project to completion.

1.3 Codes of Conduct and Local Associates

An architect operating internationally can take various standpoints in the face of local business customs, codes of ethics, professional standards: for example,

- He can regard the codes applicable in the UK as paramount and always to be followed whatever the local procedures.
- He can adopt the local codes and standards and not seek to adopt anything different.

It is not easy always to establish what the standards and codes of a strange country are. Its laws may be a guide but they may be silent on points that we would regard as paramount. Quite frequently, there are widespread interpretations of (and departures from) the local laws. Many countries simultaneously have two or more standards, depending on the nature of the project and the source of the funds.

In many countries, local professional associations are required by the country or funding agency. Thus in doing projects, the overseas architect is actually working with a local architect who will normally be following local customs. Although it may be possible to avoid the question by the way the work is shared, this can be another reason why the foreign architect has to depart from the standards of his own country: he will almost certainly have to do this as regards the appropriate service to fit what is needed locally and what the fee will cover. This subject is discussed further in Chapter 4.

2

Business Development

If you have been invited by a potential client to work abroad in a new country then business development is not an issue: in Case Study 8 Sir Norman Foster & Partners describe how the client sought them out as a result of knowing of their work and reputation. It is interesting though that they became familiar with Japan through working with Japanese sub-contractors on the headquarters for the Hongkong and Shanghai Bank in Hong Kong, and recognized that the Japanese construction industry suited their philosophy of close collaboration and development with the constructors of a building.

2.1 *Step 1*: Initiation

For many architects it may be a question of where to begin. I assume that you will have already gone through the process of self-examination to identify your objectives, and your strengths and weaknesses, described in many books and conferences on the subject. Weld Coxe sets out an admirably clear process in his book *Marketing Architectural and Engineering Services*[2].

We recommend joining the British Consultants Bureau (BCB), which is devoted to promoting British consultants (including architects) overseas. It will include in its *Directory of Members* a two-page synopsis of your firm which then will go to all British

1

- Identify objectives, strengths and weaknesses.
- Consider joining BCB.
- Consider DTI Enterprise Initiative consultancy advice.

↓

2

Research in UK

- Overseas Trade Services
- ODA
- RIBA
- CIRIA
- Other sources on practice in the EC
- Chambers of Commerce
- Special supplements or economic digests
- Bank reviews
- UN Agencies
- EGCI

↓

3

**Initial Appraisal
of selected country or region**

- Economy and politics
- Opportunities for work
- Finance
- Architectural Practice
- Staff

↓

4

- Mission
- Separate visit

↓

5

Full Appraisal

- Economy
- Politics
- Potential Market
- Business
- Professional
- Building industry
- Living

Figure 2 *Business development sequence.*

Embassies and High Commissions abroad; it organizes meetings (mainly in London) on opportunities for work abroad; it
arranges annual missions and seminars to countries where new
markets are developing and receives inward missions from
potential clients; and holds regular meetings with British
Ambassadors and High Commissioners, and Commercial
Officers. BCB is an invaluable source of information on
prospects and operational aspects of working overseas. It also
publishes a useful guide for the exporting consultant, covering
HMG support, the EC, the UN, the World Bank and other
Development Banks, and EFCA, with contact information[3].

At this stage you may find it useful to obtain DTI Enterprise
Initiative consultancy advice in export marketing and business
planning. Although intended primarily for exporters of goods,
this service (subsidized for small firms) may be helpful. Contact
may be made through your nearest regional DTI office.

2.2 *Step 2*: Research in the UK

Having identified the country (or region) in which you would
like to work the next step is to collect in the UK background
information on the country or region concerned:

(a)   Overseas Trade Services
The UK government has brought together the services to export
of DTI and FCO in one secretariat which covers the following:

- Export Market Information Centre. This is a self-help research
  and library system in London, covering trade statistics, market
  research reports, overseas trade directories, development
  plans and export opportunities, country profiles and sector
  reports.
- Export Intelligence Service. This is contracted out to Export
  Opportunities Ltd who send brief notices of information
  matching your profile of interest (by fax, post or electronic
  mail). In practice RMJM have found the information available
  from this service mainly of use for a preliminary assessment of
  market potential rather than for identifying prospects. See
  contact address in Appendix D.
- Projects and Exports Policy Division (PEP). This includes the

World Aid Section of DTI with details of more than 5000 current projects funded by MDAs, procedural guidelines, tender notices and organizational listings. It also administers ATP-TC and OPF funds. See Section 5.7: also contact addresses in Appendix D.

- Export Marketing Research Scheme. This consists of subsidized market research by specialists, or by your in-house market researcher, administered by the LCCI for the London/Thames/Chiltern Region and DTI regional offices elsewhere.
- Export Development Adviser. He provides specialist advice on exporting, mainly on commercial and business aspects, administered as for the previous scheme.
- Market Information Enquiry Service. This is a paid report on a particular market carried out by the Diplomatic Service Post overseas, usually taking a month.
- Export Representative Service. This is a paid report by the Post overseas on finding a local representative, similar to the previous scheme.
- Overseas Status Report Service. This is a paid report by the Post overseas on commercial status (not credit-rating) of an overseas company.
- Country Desk Officers. These are DTI staff who can advise on particular markets and local trading conditions.
- Export publications including:
  Hints to exporters (for most countries)
  Country profile (Europe and large countries elsewhere)
  Selective sector report (e.g. on the legal system in the USA, doing business in Japan, and reconstructing Kuwait).
- Regional Advisory Groups (e.g. COMET for the Middle East, SEATAG for South-east Asia).

You can make initial contact through your nearest regional DTI office, except where otherwise indicated.

(b)   Overseas Development Administration
ODA have a substantial programme of bilateral aid to developing countries, within which there are opportunities for architects. Their booklet *British Overseas Aid: Opportunities for Business* contains information about multilateral as well as bilateral aid programmes, with criteria used for project selection and names and addresses of contacts in the UK and overseas[4].

The British Bilateral Aid Programme in 1989 included the following expenditure (in £ million):

- Project Aid   190
- Aid and Trade Provision (ATP)   51
- Technical Cooperation   420

Bilateral aid is largely tied to procurement of British goods and services including feasibility studies.

If you have suitably qualified staff with overseas experience you would be well advised to write to the Consultancies Section of ODA at East Kilbride summarizing your expertise and seeking registration, after which you may be asked to complete a detailed registration form, from which you would be considered for suitable contracts. See contact address in Appendix D.

(c)   The Royal Institute of British Architects
The RIBA has a number of services which are relevant:

- Publication of its *International Directory of Practices* in which your firm should be included if you are interested in overseas work.
- Listing of about 5000 overseas members world-wide (mostly in the Commonwealth and the USA) who may be useful points of contact abroad.
- Maintenance of information on practice in some overseas countries including the local equivalent of the RIBA, fee scale and codes.
- The Clients' Advisory Service deals with requests from overseas clients mainly for work in the UK but occasionally for work overseas, so you should register your interest and experience with it.
- Publication of reports for a number of European countries:
  France
  Spain
  Portugal
  Germany
  Italy
  These reports cover the background to the development process and building control procedures, the professional role of architects, and opportunities for UK practitioners.
- Membership of ACE (Architects Council for Europe), a body which deals with liaison with other European equivalents of

the RIBA, EC Directives etc., reported in the Practice Section of the monthly *RIBA Journal*.

- Membership of IUA.
- Membership of the Commonwealth Association of Architects (CAA) which publishes a Handbook of Member Institutes, and carried out in 1985 an interesting survey *Issues in Architectural Practice* covering restrictions on practice in Commonwealth countries.

(d)   CIRIA European Construction Industry Guides (which complement the RIBA reports referred to above):

- France
- Iberia
- Germany (pre-unification)
- Italy
- Belgium and Luxembourg

(e)   Other sources on practice in the EC

There is a continuous stream of articles and reports on opportunities and practice in the EC, from varying standpoints, in the run-up to the full operation of the single market by the end of 1992, including:

- *Engineering consultancy in all 12 EC countries* (published by Thomas Telford Ltd for the Association of Consulting Engineers).
- *Building Services consultancy in all 12 EC countries, EC standards and legislation* (published by BSRIA).
- CCMI market reports including the Netherlands, Hungary and the former East Germany.
- NEDC's *Gateway to Europe*, a market guide for the contracting and building materials industry.
- Articles in the technical press.

New information is published nearly every week so I do no more than indicate the principal sources here.

(f)   Chambers of Commerce

Your local Chamber of Commerce (particularly the LCCI in London) will be worth joining where it has Export Clubs, meetings and missions concerned with the country or region you wish to work in.

(g)   Special Supplements, County Reports or Economic Digests for example in or published by:

- *The Times*
- *The Financial Times*
- *The Daily Telegraph*
- *The Economist*
- *The Guardian*
- *The Independent*.

(h) Bank Reviews; for example:

- Barclays Bank *Country Reports* worldwide, which are updated annually.
- Hongkong and Shanghai Bank *Business Profiles* for countries in the Pacific Rim, Asia and the Middle East.

(i)   Research Reports, for example:

- *Trade from Aid* – a detailed guide to new EC/Lomé – IV contracts in 69 African, Caribbean and Pacific States (published by Business International).

(j)   United Nations Agencies

- World Bank
  Development Business (published fortnightly)
  Monthly Operational Summary of Proposed Projects
  Annual Reports
- Asian Development Bank
  Business Opportunities (published monthly)
- Inter-American Development Bank
- African Development Bank
- United Nations Development Programme
- UN subsistence rates (world-wide).

(k)   The Export Group for the Construction Industry (EGCI)

- Advice on British contractors working overseas.

2.3 *Step 3*: Initial Appraisal

From this information an initial appraisal of the country concerned may now be made covering a number of factors:

(a) Economy and Politics

- Political and financial stability
- Strength of economy
- Strength of trading links with the UK and the country concerned.

(b) Opportunities for work

- National development plan priorities
- Opportunities for appropriate architectural work in the public and private sectors.

(c) Finance

- Exchange control regulations
- Local taxes and availability of Double Taxation Agreements.

(d) Architectural Practice

- Strength of local architectural profession
- The necessity for local associate architects
- Freedom for expatriate firms to practise.

(e) Staff

- Living conditions for expatriates
- Ability for individuals to remit local earnings.

In general terms the appraisal of all these factors should be favourable. While an adverse evaluation of one or more of these factors does not necessarily rule the country out, you need to recognize the risks involved in working there.

2.4 *Step 4*: Mission

(a) Mission
If your initial appraisal is favourable an exploratory visit should be made to the country. There is considerable benefit in joining an outward mission to take advantage of the DTI subsidies offered, and the local briefing and meetings which form part of the programme.

Depending on timing and the country to be visited, you may be able to choose between one organized by the BCB and one organized by a Chamber of Commerce. The BCB mission will have the advantage of being focused on opportunities for consultants, and providing interaction with other professional members: but may not suit your programme and destination. On the other hand, there may be more frequent Chamber missions (and you will be able to join one even if you are not a member of the Chamber) with a better chance of suiting your timetable and destination, and you will have the benefit of a wider range of commercial mission members.

Usually, once abroad, you will have time within the programme to follow up leads independent of the mission, or you can extend your visit to do this if necessary.

(b)   Separate visit

Alternatively, you can undertake a separate visit to make your assessment on the spot and to follow up leads obtained from your earlier research. Apart from the usual travel arrangements you should make some preparations in advance:

- Check local weekends which may be part of Thursday and Friday in a Muslim country.
- Avoid local national and school holidays (for example, Ramadan and the Hadj in Muslim countries and the Chinese New Year in South-east Asia). Also August seems to be a month when officials from tropical countries travel to Europe!
- Prepare introductory brochure material on your firm to hand out on your visit, preferably in the language of the country to be visited.
- In certain cases consider having business cards with translation on the back into the language of the country being visited (e.g. Arabic, Japanese).
- Take headed notepaper for making submissions locally.
- Book into a hotel with a business centre where you can get letters etc. typed, and a fax or telex service back to your home office.
- Take a list of as many specific project leads and introductions as you can.

(c)   Once abroad here are some suggestions from our experience:

- Allow enough time to get over jet lag (at least as much time as spent travelling) before making calls or attending meetings.
- Visit the Commercial Secretary at the British Embassy or High Commission first of all, with specific questions on leads or aspects you wish to pursue. He is invariably helpful, and will be able to suggest contacts, and possibly arrange meetings for you. Leave copies of your brochure for the embassy's reference library.
- Consider including among your calls:
    - The local British Council resident representative for information on education projects
    - The local equivalent body to the RIBA to discuss professional aspects
    - A local architect recommended by the RIBA, the local equivalent body or the local Post overseas, bearing in mind the contribution which a Local Associate can make (see Section 4.3)
    - A local lawyer recommended by the local Post overseas
    - A local accountant, either at a branch of your accountants in the UK, or their correspondent accountant, or another recommended by the local Post
    - The manager of a branch, if any, of your bank in the UK, or local bank recommended by the local Post.
- Collect information on local living costs, building costs, recreational opportunities, restrictions or hardships.

2.5 *Step 5*: Appraisal

From your mission and earlier research you should now be in a position to appraise the following aspects and trends:

(a)   Economic

- Strength of economy, basis of exports
- Balance of payments
- National budget finance
- External aid sources
- Inflation.

(b)   Political

• Stability.

(c)   Potential market

• National Development Plan priorities
• Allocations to building sectors
• International client investment.

(d)   Business

• Are foreign firms welcome?
• Exchange control
• Language
• Taxation (for firms and individuals)
• Double taxation relief
• Communications.

(e)   Professional

• Local Associate and/or Agent required by law or advisable
• Similarly, the degree of participation by local architects (i.e. indigenization)
• Competition from the UK and other foreign countries.

(f)   Building industry

• Local capability
• International presence (especially British)
• Availability of materials and equipment
• Local building costs.

(g)   Living

• Local living conditions for expatriates
• Accommodation
• Cost of living
• Social and recreational scene
• Effect of climate.

From this appraisal you should be able to decide whether to proceed further, particularly with any specific job opportunities which you may have identified.

3

MDA-Funded Projects

3.1 Project Cycle

If you are interested in Multilateral Development Aid-funded projects (for developing countries as already indicated) it is important to understand the project cycle through which a project goes and where any consultancy appointment is made at each stage. For example, the World Bank procedure (largely followed by other Development Banks) is as follows (see Figure 3):

- *Identification* of the project as suitable for Bank funding usually by the country concerned, sometimes with consultancy assistance.
- *Preparation* of the project (to prepare the brief and identify the technical, institutional, economic and financial conditions necessary to achieve its objectives) by the country or the Bank (often with consultancy help).
- *Appraisal* of the project by the Bank (sometimes using consultants) to ensure that it is soundly prepared.
- *Negotiation* of the project by the country with the Bank.
- *Implementation* and supervision of the project by the country with consultancy assistance.
- *Evaluation* of the completed project by the Bank, to feed relevant lessons into the next project.

Refer for more detail to Warren Baum's *The Project Cycle*[5].

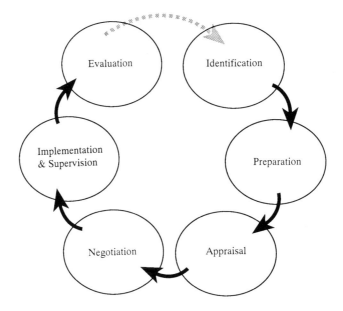

Figure 3 *The World Bank project cycle.*

3.2 Project Types

Projects will basically be of two kinds:

- *Loans* by the Development Bank to the country concerned, where the decision on the appointment is made in that country from a shortlist of registered consultants prepared jointly by the executing agency in the country and the Bank.
- *Technical assistance* by the Bank to the country where the decision on the appointment is made by the Bank from a shortlist of registered consultants.

3.3 Registration

If you wish to be considered for an appointment you must first register with the Development Bank by completing the lengthy Data on Consultants (DACON) form (or alternative form for individuals). This is normally done by post as you need access to information in your office to complete it. The European Bank for Reconstruction and Development has at the time of publication not got further than inviting consultants to send in brochures and register interest in projects.

3.4 Visit

It is advisable to visit the Bank, having first studied their Operational Summary and identified projects you wish to pursue and the names of the project officers.

- Arrange a meeting with the UK Representative or Delegate to the Bank (via the British Embassy) for advice on policy and structure of the Bank, prospects and contacts.
- Obtain a telephone directory of the Bank for room numbers and extensions and identification of individual responsibilities (e.g. by country or sector).
- Arrange meetings with officers in the Bank by telephone (possibly with the assistance of the embassy) as without these it is impossible to get past the security men at the entrance. Project officers are influential in drawing up shortlists, often without initially consulting the central register.
- Once inside the Bank it is usually easy to arrange meetings with other officers by internal phone, but less easy to locate their office in the maze of corridors and lifts!
- Check with the registry that your registration is up to date with the latest brochures at the ready to supplement it.
- Confirm interest in projects in writing both with the Bank's project officer and the executing agency in the country.

This procedure may seem cumbersome but has proved essential in our experience at the World Bank in Washington, the Asian Development Bank in Manila, the African Development Bank in Abidjan, the European Community in Brussels, UNESCO in Paris and the Arab Bank for Economic Development in Khartoum.

It must be said that although the sums loaned by Development Banks are enormous, much of the money is now allocated to institutional support, or rescheduling earlier loans, and less than in recent years is allocated to capital projects. Much of the architectural work is done by local architects. However, there is a need for individual expatriate architects to prepare briefs, design and supervise housing, schools, universities, hospitals, clinics, and buildings for transportation, power and tourism.

The major part of architectural work for Development Banks lies in implementation and supervision and in these cases consultancy appointments are made by the executing agency in the country concerned: thus visits there are essential in order to get registered and shortlisted.

A useful detailed guide to MDAs is set out in Volume One of *The International Consultant's Manual*[6]. Reference should also be made to the *Guidelines for the use of consultants* published by the World Bank[7]. Similar publications are also published by other Development Banks. The British Embassy in Washington also publishes useful guidelines about how the World Bank works with advice on sources of more detailed information and intelligence[8].

4

Codes of Conduct and Local Associates

4.1 Comparative Practice

It is worth comparing the position of the architect (and other professionals) in countries with high- and low-income economies:

High income	Low income

(a) *Professional service and its cost*

- Most clients understand the role that professionals play in looking after their interests as distinct from master/servant or buyer/ seller in the market.

- Most clients know what service they want, and how much it will cost.

- Most clients (especially in the public sector) understand the importance of professional services in giving value for money.

- The concept of professional service is not understood.

- There is a lack of understanding of what professionals do, or its cost.

- Cheapest must be best as in a bazaar or Dutch auction.

High income	Low income

(b)   *Codes of conduct*

- Strict professional codes of conduct with penalties for non-compliance.
- No codes of conduct with corruption and bribery accepted as part of the way of life.

(c)   *Environmental quality*

- The quality of the physical environment, and standards of proficiency in designing it, are generally recognized.
- The quality of the physical environment has no importance beyond the minimum provision of shelter and basic utilites, or conspicuous ostentation.
- Acceptance of minimum functional and technical standards of design – enforceable by law and regulation.
- Only partial standards of design, or regulations.

(d)   *Availability of skilled people*

- Abundance of technical and administrative skills to ensure that regulations are enforced and standards are met.
- Desperate shortage of skills and procedures.

The relative positions between these extremes of the UK and of another country in which you may be working may well alter (both up and down) and you will need to assess these positions in deciding whether to accept a commission, and the appropriate fee for it.

In certain countries the concept of a fee based on building value and an acceptable standard of service and plan of work may be inappropriate. The relationship between building cost and design cost can vary from place to place, or from year to year, in a rapidly developing economy. It may be difficult to reach an understanding with a potential client on the service to be provided, and the appropriate fee for it, often in competition.

4.2 Corruption

This is a fundamental aspect of working overseas which needs to be recognized. In many countries local officials are poorly paid and expect to make up their salaries to a living level by the granting of favours (at a price). This is endemic from the issue of customs clearance certificates at one end of the scale to political contributions and awarding contracts at the other.

Corruption may work the other way too. I recall my first contact with an Arab client when I visited a Saudi prince in London whose house was an Aladdin's cave of rich artefacts pouring out of treasure chests. An experienced colleague warned against complimenting the prince on the splendour of these objects, which would have resulted in the generous gift of one of them, and a consequent open-ended obligation on my part to be of service to the prince.

British consultants are recognized internationally as having the highest standards of professional integrity, and often win work for the trust and impartiality which this implies. However, the Codes of Conduct issued by RIBA and ARCUK are not altogether appropriate overseas.

It is instructive to compare how other codes deal with corruption. The Codes issued by the AIA[9] and the ICC[10] are useful here.

(a)   The AIA Code prohibits the use of gifts in connection with prospective projects but acknowledges that political contributions may be made in compliance with applicable laws.

(b)   The ICC Rules of Conduct

- Prohibit bribes to obtain business.
- Require remuneration to agents to match the services rendered and not be passed on as a bribe.
- Allow contributions to political parties or committees or to individual politicians provided they accord with the applicable local law, with any publicity the law requires.

In most countries (not excepting the UK) patronage often implies a mutual exchange of favours and the dividing line between acceptable patronage and corruption is a fine one. Business gifts and entertainment need careful judgement to accord with local cultural expectations and social etiquette.

A solution to these problems abroad lies in the appointment of a reputable Local Associate who can be relied on to follow the local professional and business codes of conduct: or, to quote a former Senior Partner in RMJM, "When in Rome, let the Romans do it".

Both you and your Local Associate may well incur costs related to services carried out before the project has been secured. These can reasonably be reimbursed after the project has been awarded (for example, in the form of a commission) provided that they do not include bribes or inducements to influence the award.

Corruption and patronage are discussed in some depth in *The International Consultant's Manual* [6].

4.3 Local Associates

(a)   You would be well advised to form an association with a local architectural practice, where a suitable practice exists, and this may well be required under the indigenization decrees of the host country, setting out the extent of local participation in companies. Local Associates have much to contribute:

- Understanding of local customs, politics and attitudes.
- Interpretation and translation to and from the local language.
- Understanding of local professional practice, and codes of conduct.
- Understanding and practice of payment of political contributions.
- Knowledge of local business opportunities.
- Assistance in presentation to clients.
- Economic drawing office capability.
- Knowledge of the local building industry and building costs.
- Knowledge of requirements for conformity to planning and building control procedures and signing of submissions.
- Help in to processing fee payments and bonding procedures.

In some countries the question does not arise as local practices do not exist. For example, in Case Studies 11 and 5 the Aden project was carried out by RMJM off-shore, while for the Tripoli Museum it was necessary to set up a local office, as a branch office of RMJM in the UK. On the other hand, in the case of the UNESCAP Conference Centre (Case Study 6) the project was secured, designed and is being administered in contract by a Joint Venture company set up by RMJM with a local firm of Thai architects before the project was identified.

(b) The process of finding a Local Associate should be done with as much care as finding a partner or associate in the UK. You will need to consider the matching of architectural and business objectives, mutual liking and trust, as well as the professional and business standing of the firm concerned. It is likely that your association will progress through a number of stages, with an exchange of letters or written agreement at each stage:

(1) Statement of willingness and intention to identify and work together on any suitable project perhaps within defined sectors (e.g. education, health, tourism) when identified by either party: this implies a principle of first refusal.
(2) As (1) but related to a specific project. Some potential clients may wish to nominate particular local firms with which to associate.
(3) Joint Venture agreement for any projects secured in a country.

Initially your Local Associate may also have similar agreements with other architects and this should be made known to you and to them. However, if you jointly win and carry out projects successfully the association can progress to a later stage in this sequence. Such a procedure enables you and your Associate to get to know and trust each other with break points for mutual disengagement.

(c) It is worth distinguishing between the sharing of the following aspects between you and your Local Associate:

• Professional input on a project. This will be dependent on the number of team members needed (or affordable) from either party at each stage (both before and after contract). This enables the most effective professional service to be provided to the client.

- Profit (or loss) on a project. This may be proportional to input, or to shareholding in the association, or on some other agreed formula.
- Profit (or loss) on the association, on the annual aggregate of profits (or losses) on the projects carried out by it, usually in proportion to the share-holding of each party. This will be the element subject to tax in the country of registration of the association, and may be subject to certain limits according to local legislation. For example, in Thailand (Case Study 6) the local participation had to be at least 50%.

Generally it is sensible for the firm with the largest share of the professional input to provide the leadership for the project.

(d)   Agreements with Local Associates
Agreements should be made in advance to cover the following:

- Conformity with the law of the land.
- Conformity with the relevant codes of professional conduct, which may include agreement not to offer inducements nor to pay for advertisements, nor take any action that might lead to an abuse of trust.
- Agreement to declare to one another and to clients any possible conflict of interest, where necessary revealing copies of any relevant agreements.
- Method and timing of payment relating broadly to the amount of work required and the extent of services provided.
- Range of services to be provided.
- Exclusive agreement on both sides for the project.
- That the association must be revealed to the client.
- That the Local Associate is not a direct participant in the award of the project.

(e)   Once you have secured a project, an inter-firm agreement will be needed. See Section 6.3.

4.4 Agent/Representative

In some countries an expatriate firm must have an Agent/ Representative, for example to take responsibility for any administrative or post-contractual liabilities which might arise after the expatriate firm had left the country on completion of the contract. While the roles of Local Associate and Agent/Representative can be combined there may be countries where no suitable Local Associate can be found. The role of Agent/Representative is discussed further in Section 6.2.

5

Winning the Job

The procedure for winning a job may follow as many routes as it does in the UK, but here I concentrate on the normal method preferred by MDAs as, with some variants, it is the one most frequently adopted overseas.

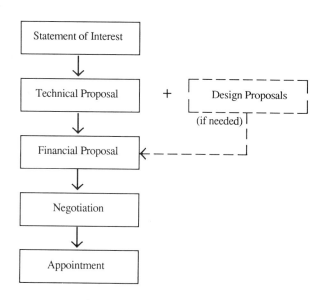

Figure 4 *Winning sequence.*

5.1 Statement of Interest

Once a project or potential client has been identified, a statement of interest or capability should be submitted (preferably presented in person) to the project officer on lines similar to the UK. It is helpful to indicate at this stage how you intend, or are able, to satisfy any local professional or commercial requirements, for example by indicating the name of your agent, or whether you intend to associate with a local firm, or to set up a local branch office to carry out the work.

You need to see that frequent personal contact is maintained with the client to ensure that your name is on the shortlist. This is an important task for your Local Associate.

5.2 Submission

Once shortlisted, it is likely that you will need to make a submission, preferably in two parts, the so-called "two-envelope" system. The first contains the technical proposal, the second the financial bid for the cost of carrying out the services described in the technical proposal. Under MDA procedures the financial bid is only opened once the assessment and ranking of technical proposals has been completed. At this stage you should prepare an outline agreement with any associated firms including your Local Associate. (See Section 6.3.)

5.3 Technical Proposal

The technical proposal should be prepared with great care and clarity, carefully following the terms of reference issued by the client. It will probably cover:

- Programme and method of work.
  This will require a creative interpretation of the terms of reference and the timescale and resources needed to meet them.

- Relevant experience of your firm, and of other associated firms, both expatriate and local.
- CVs of principal team members, both expatriate and local. These are crucial (especially the team leader) as they will be closely examined as to suitability for the tasks to be carried out, and named staff will be expected by the client to be available for the project if secured (even though the start date may not have been stated). Many clients are very reluctant to accept substitutions, because of unsatisfactory past experience of firms winning projects with promised staff and then substituting less experienced people, and because of the financial implications (see Section 5.6 on negotiations).

In assessing technical proposals it is common for clients to allocate points to different aspects. For example, on a project in Zambia the African Development Bank listed the following selection criteria in the Terms of Reference:

- Understanding of Terms of Reference   15%
- Overall quality of proposal, work plan
  and methodology   20%
- Knowledge of project's environment   15%
- Experience on similar projects   15%
- Professional reputation of firms   10%
- Ability to deal with local personnel
  and agencies   5%
- Qualifications of experts and expertise in
  field of assignment   20%
                                          _____
                                           100%

The Local Associate's participation in preparing the proposal is important if high scores are to be achieved.

5.4 Design Proposals

At this stage a design, a design approach or design ideas may also be required. You will need to decide whether to agree to this (see cautionary tale in Section 7.7), but it is becoming common practice (outside MDA-funded projects).

5.5 Financial Proposal

(a) This is a critically important document as it will form the basis for negotiation if you are ranked first in the technical appraisal. It will need to match the programme and staff loading, with figures that can be justified from your office accounts. You should, if possible, discover (through your Agent or Local Associate) the quantum of the budget which the client has for the project in order to assess what is likely to be a winning bid.

(b) The Financial Submission may take several forms:

- Lump sum comprising a fixed price fee made up of quantities and unit prices (for evaluation of additional services and subject to annual review of rates). In preparing this you will need to list and price all risks very carefully.
- Time-based fees for named or unnamed staff calculated on the basis of home salary plus social charges. This needs to be accompanied by an estimate of time, subject to reasonable review.
- Percentage fee of building costs (with schedule of time-based charges for additional services). This needs careful pricing of risks, local building costs and estimate of inflation.
- Net cost plus a fee (either fixed sum or fixed percentage of net cost or scale percentage of net cost). This needs agreement on admissible costs and an estimate of time, subject to reasonable review.

In the first three cases expenses may be included in fees, or shown as additions for reimbursement.

Fees and expenses need to be carefully calculated whichever method of fee agreement is eventually adopted. In a typical case expenses may be an additional 30% to 75% of the fees for short-term assignments or up to 150% of the fees for long-term ones. Thus expenses acquire a considerably greater significance than in the UK, where they may only be an additional 5% to 10% of the fees. (See comparisons in Figure 5).

The implications on cash flow are usually onerous, as very heavy mobilization costs are likely at the outset (for example, air flights, advance payments on leases for offices and housing,

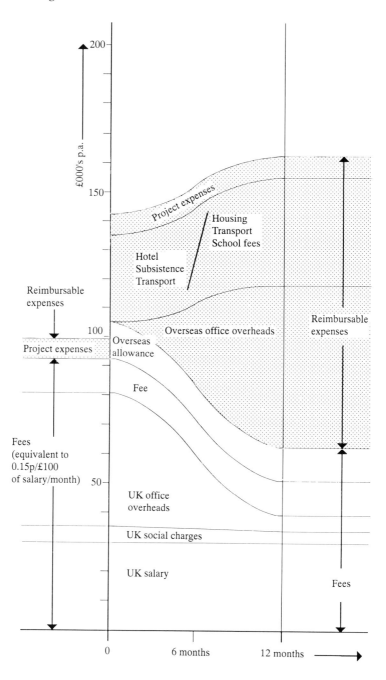

Figure 5 *Comparison of fees and expenses in the UK and overseas (based on typical time-basis charge for a senior member of staff).*

purchase of cars). Thus it is crucially important to receive adequate advance payment.

The effect of any restrictions on remittance to the UK of fees earned in the country should be carefully analysed. It is not worth doing a job if the funds needed for expenditure in the UK and profit cannot be remitted home. Equally, staff will not work abroad unless they can remit an adequate part of their earnings. In Appendix A I have summarized our experience in costing submissions, with a checklist of the headings to be covered. *The White Book* published by FIDIC contains useful comments on remuneration and payment of consultants[11].

(c) The range of reimbursable expenses (expressed in foreign and local currency as appropriate) to be covered may include:

- Foreign travel
- Staff housing for expatriates
- Other staff expenses (such as children's education, club subscriptions)
- Local office costs
- Local travel
- Hotel costs for short-term visitors
- *Per-diem* costs (food, laundry, etc.) for short-term visitors.

It will be seen that considerable local information is needed to assess these costs. For a fuller list of headings see Appendix A.

It will also be seen that a difficult balancing act may be needed to produce a credible and viable financial proposal to meet all these constraints, and thus a good period of time for preparation should be allowed. At this point careful allowance should be made for possible risks and contingencies.

5.6 Negotiation

Assuming that you have been ranked first on the basis of your technical submission you will now be invited to negotiate on the basis of your financial proposal. Under MDA procedures if your negotiation is unsuccessful the client will then start negotiation with the firm with the second ranked technical submission and so on.

Much has been written in books and articles on the process of negotiation. To these we would like to add some suggestions from our own experience:

- You should try to understand the client's culture and immediate objectives and attempt to negotiate in a way that makes him feel comfortable, and allows him to achieve some of these objectives.
- The client always needs to make some reductions in your financial bid as a matter of principle and may bring in an expert from within his organization to do this. I recall one such occasion where the expert demolished the CVs in the agreed technical proposal, even disparaging the universities where certain degrees had been obtained and when challenged as to why the CVs seemed not now to be acceptable replied "It is not a matter of their acceptability, it is how much the people are worth to us".
- Your bid should therefore include some elements which you are prepared to sacrifice, and contain some flexibility between the different headings so that you can accept these losses without damaging the profitability of the final result.
- You should agree reimbursable expenses before the fees, as the client's approach to what expenses are acceptable can materially affect the level of fees you will require.
- If you are the principal negotiator for a team including other consultants, you will need to agree in advance some flexibility or limits in the sharing of fees and expenses.
- You should never be rushed into a final position in the negotiation until you are happy with the outcome. If necessary, ask for an adjournment to consider your position and make final calculations.
- You should beware of appearing to need to refer back to the UK or to other members of the team. In some cases this may appear like lack of authority (as we found in Libya), although in others it may be undersood and be accepted as a reason for adjournment (as we found at the ADB in Manila).
- You should field two negotiators, one with experience to lead and one to observe and record. Shared views and reactions will be invaluable in working between negotiating sessions.

- You should be courteous, confident but not arrogant, and numerate.

For a fuller discussion of all the foregoing aspects covered in this chapter see Volume Two of *The International Consultant's Manual*[6].

5.7 UK Government Support

The UK government has funds to support overseas projects, and submissions for them, which may be relevant to your project:

(a) Aid and Trade Provision – Technical Cooperation (ATP-TC)
Partial grants for feasibility studies or consultancy costs for large projects in developing countries which must be:

- fully supported by the recipient country
- developmentally sound (to the recipient country)
- commercially and industrially beneficial (to the UK)
- needed to counter overseas competition in case of a single British competitor.

This scheme is jointly administered by DTI and ODA, and the limit of grant is up to between 35% and 50% of the UK content of the consultancy contract, depending on the country concerned. Soft-loan facilities are also offered on similar terms for projects which may include a consultancy element. Reference should be made to the *Guidelines for Applicants* published by the DTI[12].

(b) Overseas Projects Fund (OPF)
This scheme (administered by DTI) provides partial grant support to single British competitors for feasibility studies and consultancy costs (e.g. in preparing tender documents) for major capital projects overseas outside the EC. Capital projects should be worth over £50 million, or consultancies over £5 million. Support is limited to 50% of the consultant's costs, repayable (with a 15% premium) in the event of winning the contract. These mainly suit turnkey projects by contractors which are likely to be built quickly. Reference

should be made to the *Guidelines for Applicants* published by the DTI[13].

5.8 Competitions

One of the ways of selecting an architect is through an ideas or design competition procedure, with which most architects working in the UK are familiar. It is, for example, normal for architects for major public buildings in France and Germany to be selected in this way, and an EC Directive is in draft to extend this throughout the Community. British architects achieved great success with the 1991 biennial Europan competition, currently the largest in the world and dedicated to "the revival of social housing architecture by mobilizing young architects, by developing debates from projects and by giving access to commissioned work". However, access by British architects to future Europan competitions is in doubt because of limited government support.

The safest procedures are those contained in the IUA/ UNESCO recommendations under which competitions have been run and architects appointed for projects as diverse as the New Library of Alexandria in Egypt, the New Acropolis Museum in Greece and the Tokyo International Forum in Japan. These recommendations cover, for example:

- Type and classification
  Project/ideas/open/limited/invited/one or two phases.
- Conditions
  Purpose/brief/requirements/submission.
- Registration.
- Prize-money, compensation, honoraria.
- Copyright, insurance.
- The jury.
- Assessment procedures and awards.
- Exhibition and return of submissions.

The purpose of project competitions under these rules is to select an architect on the basis of the ideas or design submitted.

Reference should be made to the recommendations for running competitions published by UNESCO and IUA[14,15].

These recommendations are useful as a check on other international competitions as, for example, in the UNESCAP Conference Centre, Bangkok (Case Study 6). Draft rules are being prepared by the Architects Council for Europe (based on the IUA/UNESCO recommendations) for running competitions in the EC from the beginning of 1993.

If in any doubt about the acceptability of a competition (either open or invited) you should contact the RIBA competition office. The investment of your time and creative energy is too precious to expend on a competition if you are not satisfied with the fairness of the procedures proposed.

Note too the late Sir James Stirling's warnings of the dangers of a prestigious international competition, and whether the final decision is going to be made by the national leader and not by the appointed assessors. He also set out ten rules for architectural/political survival which contain salutary lessons[16].

6

Setting Up

6.1 Corporate Structure

Once you have decided to work in a foreign country you have to choose the form of corporate structure you wish to adopt for working there. This may be dependent on whether you are only working on one project, or setting up to carry out a wider range of work. Alternatives include:

- Working off-shore (i.e. in the UK or a third country) with occasional visits for liaison with local client, consultants and contractors: for example, Marine Science Laboratories, Aden (Case Study 11).
- Establishing a branch office of your UK practice: for example, Century Tower, Tokyo (Case Study 8).
- Establishing a local practice (locally registered and independent of the UK) either a partnership or company: for example, Castle Peak Power Stations and Happy Valley Racecourse Grandstands, Hong Kong (Case Studies 1 and 15).
- Setting up a separate joint venture company (locally registered) preferably with a firm matching in character, size, standing and architectural objectives: for example, UNESCAP Conference Centre, Bangkok (Case Study 6).

The decision on which alternative to adopt and the ensuing process of setting up will depend on specialist advice from lawyers and accountants in the country concerned, as well as your UK advisers, on topics such as:

- The law in the country concerned, for example, on indigenization of professional practice, and on minimum local equity requirements.
- Local tax requirements, and the existence of a Double Taxation Agreement with the UK.
- Exchange control procedures.
- Status of expatriates and their liability to tax, and ability to remit earnings.

It may be useful to set up an entity in a country on the basis of a study of the market there before identifying a particular project, as RMJM did in Thailand (Case Study 6).

6.2 Agent/Representative

As already described, in certain countries such as Saudi Arabia an expatriate organization must have an Agent to fulfil local legal requirements. This is sensible and necessary in most cases, but considerable care must be exercised in the choice. It is preferable for the agreement with an Agent to be exclusive, i.e. for him not to act for any other firm of architects.

Care is needed to define precisely the extent of an Agent's authority, since the word has different meanings in different countries. Normally an *Agent* is a fully accredited and bona fide delegate, able to make commitments on your behalf: while the lesser authority you may wish to give may be better described by the individual or firm being your *Representative*.

(a)   Services provided
Typical examples of services a local Agent/Representative can provide are:

- Advice on local customs, politics, economy and work opportunities.
- Factual information for submissions on costs and availability of living and office accommodation, furniture, equipment, labour, etc.
- Delivering submissions, and following them up.

- Legal advice on contracts, agreements, registrations, leases, employment laws, etc.
- Office and administration services: e.g. obtaining office accommodation, arranging telephone and telex connections, use of mail, telephone and telex facilities.
- Sponsorship of expatriate personnel.
- Completion of customs and immigration formalities, including obtaining visas, residential and work permits.
- Obtaining staff housing and transport.
- Introductions to doctors, nursing homes and hospitals.
- Help with progressing fee claims, bonding procedures and release, and tax clearance.

(b) Agreement

An Agreement should be drawn up with legal advice with the Agent/Representative, covering the following points:

- Date and period of Agreement.
- Names, addresses and descriptions of both parties, and of individuals to act as points of liaison.
- Description of fields of activity for cooperation, and methods or procedures for cooperation.
- Description of services to be provided by the Agent/Representative (and anything which he will not provide or do).
- Fees to be paid to the Agent/Representative and method and currency of payment (on an "if and when" basis). Expenses to lie where they fall. Legal costs of registration.
- Parties to comply with local laws, regulations and customs.
- Disclaimer of partnership, joint venture and consortium.
- Exclusivity.
- Listing of events causing automatic termination; rights of each party to terminate: *force majeure*; communications and notice.
- Disputes and arbitration.
- Agreement not to tout or solicit, and need for prior approval for any advertising or publicity. Notepaper. Copyright.
- Mutual indemnification of each party's legal and financial liabilities and insurance.
- Governing law and language; calendar.
- Declaration or removal of conflicts of interest.
- Keeping of records and right of inspection of relevant excerpts, e.g. of accounts.

(c)   Local Associate and Agent/Representative
It may be sensible for the roles of Local Associate and Agent/ Representative to be combined both for economy and to give the Local Associate a wider range of services to perform.

6.3 Inter-Firm Agreement

You need to draw up an Agreement with each of the firms of consultants on the project, both expatriate and local, covering:

- Parties, name and purpose.*
- Duties and responsibilities of each party.*
- Time-schedule and duration.*
- Allocated individuals and man months.*
- Fees and charges, timing of payments (contingent on lead consultant being paid) where paid and in what currency.
- Organization/management committee.
- Financial administration and accounting.
- Project costs, reimbursement of pre-contract expenses, method of calculating profit (or loss) and apportionment between parties.*
- Payment of local tax.
- Indemnity between parties and insurance.*
- Exchange of personnel.
- Location of work at each stage and facilities to be provided by each firm.
- Exclusivity.*
- Non-assignability.*
- Outside activities.
- Failure or insolvency of a party.*
- Governing law.*
- Method of resolving disputes and arbitration.*

Items marked * apply where the Agreement is drawn up while submitting for a project. Reference can be made to the FIDIC guidelines for agreements between consulting firms, as a useful format[17].

6.4 Client Agreement

An Agreement must be drawn up, negotiated and agreed. In many cases the client will have a Form of Agreement which will form the basis of negotiation. It will need to cover:

- Normal clauses (as in the UK).
- The services to be provided by the consultants.
  These need careful examination to avoid any possible misunderstanding later. Words such as "design", "tender" and "construction information" may need detailed explanation by reference to published documents (e.g. the RIBA *Standard Form of Agreement for the Appointment of an Architect*[18] which replaced *Architects Appointment* in 1992 and *Plan of Work*[19] or equivalent in the country concerned).
- Provision of staff, facilities, transport, etc. by the client.
- Stage payments of fees (including which currency and where paid), and procedures for late payment.
- Payment of expenses, including expatriate staff housing, office, transport, local staff, travel for expatriate staff and families (for which you should, if possible, agree monthly lump sums).
- Any exemption (e.g. to local taxes, import duty on equipment).
- Governing law.

If no form is produced by the client, the model Agreement published by FIDIC provides a useful basis for reference to similar practice by consulting engineers[20]. See also *The White Book* published by FIDIC for advice on drafting the Agreement[11].

A work group of the Architects Council of Europe is preparing a table of services as a common basis for application throughout the EC, based on the new RIBA Standard Form referred to above. It is good practice to check the Agreement with your PI insurance brokers to ensure that nothing is left uncovered.

You should be prepared for the client to interpret the Agreement literally. In Saudi Arabia in one case the client had the buildings demolished soon after completion to make way for other buildings: but he still required as-built drawings before he would release the final fee payments, as this was so stated in the Agreement!

6.5 Professional Indemnity Insurance

You will, of course, need to extend your Professional Indemnity policy to include work overseas, and ensure that all your related administrative procedures are carried out scrupulously on such projects. In our experience this has not resulted in any increase in premium – indeed the incidence of notifications or claims against the policy due to overseas works has been relatively slight. However, the climate for claims generally is getting worse as business becomes more international.

(a) In principle, Professional Indemnity needs to be considered in close relationship both to the overseas legal entity you are establishing for a project and the legal systems operating in the countries of origin of the various parties you are dealing with (client, funding agency, local authorities, contractor, sub-contractors, Local Associate, other consult-ant members of the Design Team). For example, you could have a job in Russia, for an American client, funded in Japan, with German co-consultants, a Yugoslav contractor, and Swedish sub-contractor, with the head agreement under Swiss law! The legal and insurance implications are mind-blowing.

It is preferable to avoid joint ventures with local firms, because of the danger of cross-over liability for negligence claims against the other member leading to a claim against your firm.

You may be asked by Local Associates to cover their performance on a project, for which you will need to ensure that your relevant procedures are understood and followed, but for which they should contribute to the premium. You will need to ensure that this cover is only for their work on the project, and does not extend to other projects. This will obviously be subject to your PI insurers' consent, and to any conditions they impose. You will also need to watch the form of company set up locally for your project by an overseas contractor in the event of their bankruptcy leading to a claim against you.

(b)   Fronting insurance
In some countries (such as Kenya and parts of Europe) there is a requirement for fronting insurance to be taken out locally, reinsured in the UK. This can be advantageous in providing a first line of defence against claims locally and can make jobs easier to run.

(c)   USA
It may prove difficult and costly to obtain PI insurance cover for work in the USA due to the acutely claims-conscious environment there, particularly if you set up a separate company or local office. It will be safer to set up a joint office in association with a local firm and pay for part of their local PI cover. This difficulty may extend to projects funded from the USA, or for an American client, elsewhere overseas, due to their propensity for suing in courts in the USA.

(d)   EC
Architects' liability for projects in the EC is going to be affected by a Directive under preparation in Brussels. After some confusion between two proposed Directives originating from different Directorates within the Commission it now seems likely that the so-called "Vertical (Construction Specific)" Directive being prepared by DG III will be the effective one. Its main intention is to provide speedy rectification of material damage to individual buildings without the need first to prove fault (for example, by means of a material damage insurance policy such as BILD, taken out by the developer, contractor or consultants) with a limited period of liability from completion of the project for a period of between 5 to 10 years. However, its effectiveness will depend on the scope and duration of cover provided, and whether the rights of subrogation would be waived. You will need to monitor the progress of this Directive (on which reports are given from time to time in the Practice Supplement to the *RIBA Journal*) anyway as it affects work in the UK as much as that in any country of the EC.

(e)   Personal risks
You will realize that in many developing countries overseas a client's first recourse may be to impound your Local

Representative's passport, or indeed to imprison him, in the event of a claim against you (or him) for professional negligence or error. Leaving aside the personal hazards involved, this is not a matter for PI insurance cover. The situation is more analogous to that of kidnap and ransom, against which it is possible (but expensive) to obtain cover: however, such cover is not publicized as it is feared that its existence may encourage the incidence of kidnap.

As can be seen, PI insurance overseas is potentially complex, and it is essential to consult your broker in advance of setting up or taking on work overseas, and to keep him informed of any significant developments on a project as it progresses.

7
Appropriate Design, Technology and Consultancy

7.1 Introduction

Architects working in the UK are used to designing for a particular set of climatic conditions and social criteria which almost invariably do not apply when designing buildings abroad. Careful study is needed of the different conditions which affect the building in its location.

7.2 Climate

The most important factor affecting design overseas is climate. Much of a building's character, especially in the tropics, derives from its function in modifying climate to provide shelter and comfort for human activities. An essential part of the preliminary research is to discover and understand the main climatic characteristics, both annually and diurnally:

- Solar radiation and sky conditions
- Air temperature
- Rainfall
- Relative humidity
- Wind speed and direction.

These characteristics tend to coincide with main climatic zones as illustrated for hot climates in Figure 6, reproduced from Allan Konya's *Design Primer for Hot Climates*[21]. It is interesting that a significant proportion of oil-rich and developing countries (in which many of the opportunities for work overseas exist) lie in the tropical belt (between the Tropics of Cancer and Capricorn 23½° north and south of the equator which mark the zone where at some time in the year the sun is directly overhead at noon): see Figure 1. It is also interesting that the largest growth in urbanization (with consequent implications for architectural work) lies in this zone.

Figure 7 (also reproduced from Allan Konya's book) shows the comfort zone between 22° and 27°C and 20% and 80% relative humidity, outside which the building design needs to modify the natural environment. Special attention should be given to the local microclimate, topography, the proximity of the seas, rivers or lakes, seasonal changes such as monsoons and dust storms, and diurnal changes.

It is important to orientate and shade buildings carefully (to exclude or encourage sun penetration as appropriate). Landscaping near the building can play a major part in modifying the microclimate just outside and inside buildings.

Although air conditioning has revolutionized building design (and made it more international) it is preferable to design as far as possible for the optimum modification of climatic conditions by the building itself (particularly in developing countries) both to conserve energy and to provide a fail-safe solution during power interruptions.

From this analysis characteristic types of building design tend to emerge in similar climatic zones. In hot-dry zones buildings have heavy walls and flat roofs, small external openings, courtyards with fountains and greenery (as, for example, in Case Study 5 in Libya). Hassan Fathy describes the principles of architectural thermodynamics, design for a comfortable microclimate and typical solutions in the Arab world (such as *mashrabīya, malqaf, bādgīr, takhtabūsh* and *salsabīl* in his book *Natural Energy and Vernacular Architecture*[22]. The use of *mashrabīya* (or *rowshans*, as they are called locally) is well illustrated in Case Study 7 in Jeddah.

In hot-humid zones buildings are lightly constructed, raised off the ground, with pitched roofs and large overhangs to throw

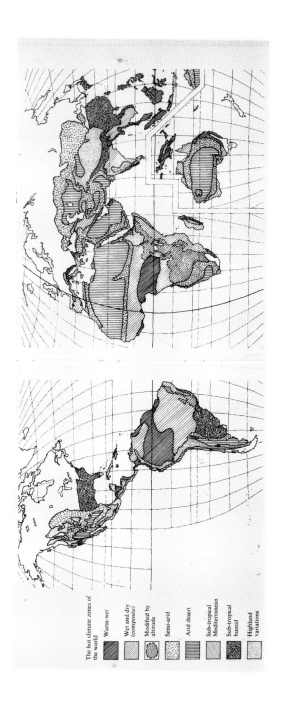

Figure 6 *World hot climate zones. By courtesy of Allan Konya.*

off the rain, and large external openings angled to catch the breeze (as, for example, in Sri Lanka in Case Study 9). In Mbeya Hospital, Tanzania (Case Study 2), Norman & Dawbarn have designed for maximum cross-ventilation to maintain comfort in wards, and avoided lifts so that patient care and comfort can continue even if power supplies break down.

Information on local climate may be obtained from the Meteorological Office, depending on the availability of statistics. The Meteorological Office maintains the National Meteorological Library which can be consulted: alternatively, the Office can research climatic data in their records for a fee, or recommend

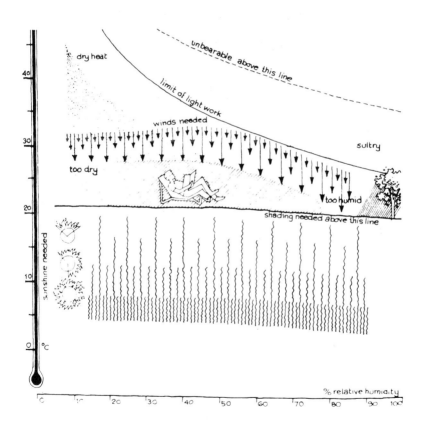

Figure 7 *Schematic diagram of personal comfort zone (shaded) from Victor Olgyay's bioclimate chart. By courtesy of Allan Konya.*

the appropriate national meteorological service for you to consult. See contact address in Appendix D.

7.3 Natural Hazards

The UK is fairly free of natural hazards: this is, however, not the case overseas as there are a number of extreme physical or climatic phenomena which can damage or even destroy a building and imperil its occupants. These include:

- Earthquakes
- Volcanic action
- Expansive clay soils
- Sinking ground
- Hurricanes
- Typhoons
- Tidal waves
- Hailstorms
- Lightning
- Sand storms
- Insect infestation
- Termite attack.

Some information on these hazards and how to design for them is contained in Allan Konya's *Design Primer*[21], in BRE's Digest 302 on *Building Overseas in Warm Climates*[23], and in BRE's *Overseas Building Notes*[24].

Century Tower, Tokyo (Case Study 8) illustrates Sir Norman Foster & Partners' innovative solution to the problem of earthquakes from which the design derives its characteristic appearance: while in Mbeya Hospital, Tanzania (Case Study 2) Norman & Dawbarn mitigate the seismic risk by a single-storey pavilion design. The problem of typhoons was recognized by RMJM in Castle Peak Power Stations, Hong Kong (Case Study 1) in the robustness of detailing of roof and cladding. The sinking ground of Bangkok put a constraint on the approach to basements and detailing of the perimeter at ground level in the UNESCAP Conference Centre (Case Study 6).

7.4 Sociology

When designing overseas buildings you need to gain a good understanding of the people for whom you are designing and their culture. Factors to be considered include:

• Social status and grouping
• The place of women in society
• Religious observance
• Dietary restrictions
• Koranic symbolism
• *Feng-shui* (the Chinese art of geomancy).

The SBB buildings, Saudi Arabia (Case Study 12) provide an example of the effect of Islam on design where special areas were required for counting cash, separate areas were needed for women, and prayer rooms had to be orientated to Mecca.

Castle Peak Power Stations, Hong Kong (Case Study 1) illustrate the design problems created by the *Feng-shui* of the site and its effect on the neighbouring village. *Feng-shui* (meaning wind-water in Chinese) is related to the geographical features of the site and their effect on the design of a building in relation to location, orientation, planning and construction. For a fuller account of the history and practical implications of *Feng-shui* see Evelyn Lip's *Chinese Geomancy*[25].

You will need to understand the way business is done. It is alien (if not offensive) to go straight to the point in Arab or Oriental cultures. The amenities of social intercourse, light conversation, and consumption of beverages are often seen as an essential prelude to doing business (but beware of drinking before your host in Indonesia!).

Up to a point, some of these aspects can be learnt from books and from briefing courses such as those run by Farnham Castle (see Section 9.7). However, your Local Associate will have a vital contribution to make in identifying relevant factors, and their importance to the design and management of the project.

7.5 International versus National Style

We are no strangers to the battle of architectural styles in the UK; a similar battle is being fought overseas, but with different manifestations. On the one hand, there is a trend towards a universal international style, either because of the ambition of developing countries to emulate the leading developed countries, or because of the globalization of culture brought about by transnational conglomerates (such as Shell and Coca-Cola). On the other hand, many countries want to establish a national identity and to develop a related national style of architecture, in preference to following the international trend.

This is a basic question to discuss with your client and one which may affect the time taken by the design process. The combined experience of local and expatriate architects is an important ingredient in arriving at the appropriate design. Many national styles are still at a very formative stage and subject to fierce local debate, as, for example, in Malaysia. The design for the new air terminal in Kota Kinabalu by RMJM (Case Study 4) was deliberately international, while others being designed and built in parallel by other architects (in Kuching and Penang) echoed the regional characteristics of traditional Malay houses. At the same time, RMJM's design for a new management training centre in the mountains near Kota Kinabalu fitted its site more harmoniously by adopting typically Malay roof sections.

A study of existing old buildings may be misleading. For example, in Jeddah (Case Study 7) the buildings we were trying to conserve were largely the product of the earlier Ottoman occupation, a period which some of the local inhabitants were anxious to forget. Similarly, in Sri Lanka, comfortable buildings with wide verandahs are distrusted as a prototype for the future because of their strong colonial associations with the Portuguese, Dutch and British. The archetype of the traditional dwelling may not be suitable for expanding into the larger-scale design required to meet the brief for large organizations.

Century Tower, Tokyo (Case Study 8) is an example of successful international design by Sir Norman Foster & Partners who were employed by the client as leaders in this field. In the

SBB buildings, Saudi Arabia (Case Study 12) on the other hand, RMJM's brief was to produce a national house-style for a new organization (and indeed a new building type) for an important developing country.

Mbeya Hospital, Tanzania (Case Study 2) is an example of a simple design solution closely related to traditional buildings, which Norman & Dawbarn persuaded their clients was preferable to an "international" design, and offered better value for money. In UNESCAP Conference Centre, Bangkok (Case Study 6) the design by RMJM and M L Tri Devakul tries to reflect the characteristic roof forms of the region which the Conference Centre serves, particularly those of Thailand where the building is located.

7.6 Appropriate Technology

It is in the construction of a building overseas that the most differences from work in the UK become apparent, and the greatest divergence occurs between one overseas country and another. Your Local Associate and other local consultants will have particularly useful advice from their experience of the building process in the country, including local costs.

You will need to find out how the local building industry in the country concerned is organized: whether there are local contractors capable of building your design, or if there are experienced and reliable foreign contractors used to operating there. For example, in the Air Terminal, Kota Kinabalu (Case Study 4) there were no local contractors capable of building a project of this scale and technical complexity and the contract was awarded to a contractor from West Malaysia. You will need to discover if the local building industry is labour-intensive or capital-intensive. For example, in Saudi Arabia we found that the Saudis themselves regarded building work as undignified but were reluctant to bring in "guest-workers".

The availability and skills of local craftsmen must be investigated. In Thailand (Case Study 6) there are many skills available, for example in concrete formwork, tiling and joinery. In Aden (Case Study 11) the winning tender was from a Chinese contractor from the PRC using imported Chinese labour.

You will need to research the availability of local building materials and components. In East Malaysia, for example (Case Study 4) apart from aggregates available from a small number of quarries already overloaded by other building work, everything had to be imported into the island, through a small nearby port. In Tanzania (Case Study 2) the situation was similar with the additional complication of a 700 km journey by road or rail from the nearest port, so materials and components had to be pre-ordered before the contractor was appointed to ensure that the programme could be carried out.

Appropriate building standards need investigation. In the PRC, for example (Case Study 13) RMJM specified BS or DIN standards with which we were familiar for high-risk components (windows and cladding), and JIS standards for low-risk items such as sanitary ware.

A useful source of information and advice is Technical Help to Exporters, a service provided by the British Standards Institute. THE holds over 10 000 English translations of foreign standards, regulations, codes of practice, testing and certification requirements, and offers a technical translation service. Typical documents include the structure of building regulations and control in different countries, the identification of codes of practice and standards which may be needed in design, fire regulations, and French planning laws and procedures.

THE is also monitoring moves towards creating Eurocodes (to apply throughout the EC in preference to codes in force in individual member states) and towards harmonization of multinational standards and the provision of certificates of conformity of products to different national standards. Their services are chargeable, although a small amount of advice may be available free of charge, under a subsidy from the DTI. See contact address in Appendix D.

Standards of maintenance need to be understood, particularly where there may be failures of lifts or air-conditioning equipment, or of the clearance of roof gutters. These considerations were central to the design of Mbeya Hospital (Case Study 2) and CIMA, Colombo (Case Study 9).

The planning procedures to be followed will need to be understood and adequate time allowed to obtain approvals. Case Study 14 (Moscow Golf and Country Club) illustrates the escalation of bureaucratic procedures which may affect the progress of a project. On the other hand, procedures may be very precise, so that in Hong Kong, for example, an understanding of the rules for measurement of floor areas relative to plot size under the building ordinances is critical to the design of office buildings.

Local regulations for fire-fighting and means of escape must be studied, but may be inadequate for the scale of building involved. In UNESCAP Conference Centre, Bangkok (Case Study 6) GLC regulations were proposed by RMJM in the absence of adequate regulations for large buildings of public assembly, and the design was subjected to check by an independent fire consultant.

7.7 Appropriate Consultancy

(a) It is important to establish at the outset what may be described as Appropriate Consultancy: that is, the nature and extent of services to be provided appropriate to the task. In Arab countries, for example, the concept of professional service is not understood and architects are regarded more as contractors or suppliers of commodities: indeed there is no separate word for architects as distinct from engineers. Even in the UK there is widespread misunderstanding of the services which an architect can provide and of the normal sequence in the design and construction of a building, although these are fully described in RIBA publications such as *Standard Form of Agreement for the Appointment of an Architect*[18] and *The Plan of Work*[19]. However, overseas the method of work by architects may be quite different, or similar to methods current in the UK many years ago. In Nigeria and Saudi Arabia it used to be commonplace for clients to obtain free designs from architects competing for a job, get a contractor to tender and build from these designs, and employ an expatriate architect to supervise the construction and sort out any problems on site!

It goes without saying that your agreement with the client on Appropriate Consultancy at the outset is essential to the future profitability of the project. For the Jeddah Corniche (Case Study 3) the client wanted an accurate scheme design and specification for the project, which was then used to obtain competitive tenders for construction. If you have made an agreement with a Local Associate this will clearly affect the extent of your participation in a project or projects, and its profitability.

(b)   It is likely that your Agreement for projects in developing countries will contain a significant "transfer of technology", or in professional terms, exchange of experience. Local Associates or joint venture partners will expect to learn from working on the project, so that they will be able to carry out future projects of a similar nature unaided. Equally, you will gain experience in the opposite direction which can be applied to future projects in other similar countries.

In most projects funded by MDAs an identified objective is that counterpart staff should learn new techniques by working with more experienced expatriates. This is a time-consuming activity and should be taken into account in setting up the project plan, as we discovered in the Jeddah Historic Area project (Case Study 7).

Transfer of technology needs to be a positive and creative action to which resources are committed and for which staff are trained. In some cases it may be worth introducing professional training organizations to achieve effective results. Shadowing by counterpart staff is usually ineffective and should be replaced by positive and responsible incorporation of local professional staff into the team, for which separate financial resources should be earmarked.

Ultimately, overseas practice depends on your having up-to-date and relevant experience which the foreign country needs and wishes to buy: and this applies as much to stylistic approaches to design as to specialism in a technically complex building type or to project management and drawing office production techniques using computers.

7.8 Directives and Standards in the EC

Membership of the European Community impinges on the construction industry in the following main areas (and you will no doubt be keeping up to date with the situation since it applies to work in the UK):

(a) *Public Procurement*

Methods of procuring public works are laid down in the Public Works Directives of 1971 and 1989, which define which bodies have to comply, country by country. Contracts covered by these Directives include both design and execution of the works above a value threshold of 5 million ECU net of VAT. The Directives also lay down tender procedures under three main categories, open – restricted – negotiated, including notification of tenders and awards.

(b) *Professional Services*

See Section 6.5 on Professional Indemnity Insurance and Section 13.2 on recognition of qualifications.

(c) *Health and Safety*

The framework Directive governing Health and Safety (coming into force in January 1993) is aimed at improving the workplace in both public and private sectors. The related Workplace Requirements Directive (which also comes into force in January 1993) covers the physical characteristics of completed buildings affecting health and safety which have to be achieved. A Supplementary Construction Sites Directive is being prepared for adoption in 1992 which will imply responsibilities for design professionals as well as contractors for safety of buildings under construction.

(d) *Construction Standards*

The EC is moving towards rationalization of standards and Code of Practice between its member countries. A Construction Products Directive came into effect in June 1991 under which six Essential Requirements have to be satisfied by all construction products:

- Mechanical resistance and stability: avoidance of damage or collapse during construction or in use.
- Safety in case of fire: for evacuation of occupants and operations of rescue teams.
- Hygiene, health and environment: avoidance of threats to the hygiene or health of occupants or neighbours.

- Safety in use: avoidance of risk of accidents in service or in operation.
- Protection against noise: keeping noise perceived by the occupants or people nearby down to a level that will not threaten their health.
- Energy economy and heat retention: designing and building works and services systems to conserve energy in use, having regard to the climatic conditions of the location and the occupants.

Ultimately these Essential Requirements will be satisfied either by:

- Manufacture in compliance with specified harmonized CEN standards (covering all EC and EFTA countries), which will be published in the United Kingdom as identically worded British Standards: or
- Manufacture in compliance with European Technical Approvals (the European equivalent of British Board of Agrément Certificates).

(e)   *Other Directives*

There are a number of other Directives in train which affect architects working in the EC covering the award of public service contracts, competitions, communications, Environmental Impact Assessments and East–West relations.

As already mentioned, the situation is changing continuously and it is beyond the scope of this book to do more than remind you to monitor the reports which are issued regularly by the Construction Directorate DOE, the DTI, the RIBA, THE and the technical press. There are also a growing number of specialist information indexes, which catalogue and update existing Eurolegislation and the status of draft Directives and proposed legislation.

7.9 The USA and Japan

The construction industries in the USA and Japan have special characteristics which you will need to understand if you plan to work in either country, or in their spheres of influence. In the USA the architect provides conceptual design and coordinates a design team of architects and engineers for recognized work packages. Expert specialist contractors then carry out design, manufacture and construction under the coordination of a construction manager. In Japan the industry is organized into homogeneous families of contractors employing specialist sub-contractors, preplanning construction to a level similar to manufacturing cars. The architect's role is normally limited to providing the conceptual design. The industry is highly productive and concentrates on quality, safety and completion on time. Case Study 8 illustrates Sir Norman Foster & Partners' experience of working with the construction industry in Tokyo.

For a fuller description of the industries in the USA and Japan (and in Germany and France) see John Bennett's *International Construction Project Management*[26].

8

Implementation

8.1 Work Location

The location of work at different stages (here described in relation to the RIBA Plan of Work for convenience, although it may not be generally understood overseas) needs careful consideration, taking into account the following criteria:

- Proximity to client.
- Proximity to local authorities.
- Need to investigate local factors as described in Chapter 7.
- Location of members of the Design Team, both expatriate and local.
- Availability of office and studio space.
- Availability of CAD equipment, computers, specialized graphics facilities, model makers, etc.
- Proximity to contractor.
- Site presence.
- Cost effectiveness.

(a) *Stages A and B (Inception and Feasibility)*
This work will need to be carried out abroad, as it will involve key meetings with the client, and background investigation. It may extend part-way into Stage C, for greater client involvement and approval. The need to

involve other expatriate consultants (including Engineers and Quantity Surveyors) can usually be accommodated by short visits. In every Case Study this work was done overseas.

(b) *Stages C and D (Design)*
Location at this stage is probably dependent on where the team members' offices, and back-up for presentational techniques envisaged, are sited. In most Case Studies this work was done in the UK, mainly due to where other expatriate team members' offices and back-up presentational technology were located. The exceptions are Case Studies 3 and 7, where the expatriate teams were set up in Jeddah; Case Study 6, where there was a preponderance of local members of the Design Team and good back-up graphic facilities and model makers in Bangkok; and Case Studies 13 and 15, which were based on the RMJM office in Hong Kong. Client presentations were made by visiting senior representatives of the Design Team.

(c) *Stages E–H (Production Information and Tender)*
Again location is mainly determined by where the majority of design team members' offices are located and the production information technology to be used. About a third of the Case Studies show work at this stage in the UK but in most cases the work centre was abroad. In Case Studies 4, 8 and 10 the production work passed to Local Associates (or to the contractor in the case of Century Tower, Tokyo) with expatriate firms working in a more advisory capacity.

(d) *Stages J–L (Construction)*
Once the project is on site, the contract administration can be carried out most effectively either on site or from a local office. In most Case Studies this has been the case, the only exceptions being those where the assignment did not include contract administration (Case Studies 3, 9 and 10). Of these, Case Study 9 is of interest because here the key question was how to oversee and advise on the construction stage with a minimum of visits from this country.

Clearly the decision on where to locate the work centre at each stage should already have been taken in principle before preparing the Financial Submission or fee bid, as the costs involved vary significantly.

8.2 Local Office

RMJM's experience has been that local offices have often started as a single project office (sometimes paid for as a reimbursable expense under a specific project) and then subsequently have been kept on as a base for marketing locally, and used thereafter to service a number of projects.

(a)   When to establish
       The timing of the establishment of a local office and staff to work in it needs careful consideration, and depends on what services are available from any Local Associate. It should be part of the work plan for the project, and may be decided as part of the process of submission, negotiation and appointment.

- It may be paid for by the client as a reimburseable expense under the contract, in which case it should be set up as part of the mobilization for the project.
- If a Local Associate forms part of the team, the local office can be established in his office, as the most economic and convenient arrangement, again as part of the mobilization for the project.
- If neither of these alternatives is feasible, or part of the project plan, much of the work in Stages A and B can be done from a hotel bedroom, with the support of a good business centre, and local graphics office. Equally, if the main work centre for the design and production stages is in the UK, occasional visits to the country can be based in a reasonably appointed hotel. However, once a contract has been let it will probably prove necessary to establish a local office in a town near the site as a basis for contract administration.
- At the other extreme, it may be felt advisable to establish

a liaison office in the country at the outset, both for the project and for promotion of your practice in the country. Sir Norman Foster & Partners felt this to be essential in Tokyo (Case Study 8) and used it as part of the process of liaison and design development with the client and contractor from the beginning of the project.

(b) Staffing
Initially the office will need to accommodate a senior expatriate representative, with a local bilingual secretary and probably a driver/messenger, with office and studio space for visiting expatriate staff.

(c) Cost
It is likely that rent, hire of equipment, local staff, and running costs of such an office will be of the order of £50 000 per annum, and thus represent a substantial investment in local overheads. Clearly, it is preferable if this cost can be borne by a client, provided by a Local Associate, or spread over several jobs.

(d) Setting up the office
In advance of the office coming into use enough time must be allowed to set it up and make it operational, and it may be worth sending a member of administrative staff with the senior representative to do this. Tasks to be carried out will include mobilization of:

- Expatriate housing (see Chapter 9)
- Office (see Chapter 10)
- Accounting Services (see Chapter 11)
- Legal Services (see Chapter 12).

8.3 Appropriate Information

It is important to produce appropriate drawings and reports at each stage.

(a) *Stages A–D (Feasibility and Design)*
You should establish how familiar your client is with

drawings and how readily he can understand them. Often a client will listen politely to a presentation and then reveal fundamental misunderstandings (which are not unknown in the UK!). Simple sketches and models and a cartoon-like "Layman's Guide" may be much more effective. Reports may be unread, and be required purely to satisfy the wording of a contract.

(b)   *Stages E–H (Production Information and Tender)*
During the production and tender information stage it is important to prepare drawings, specifications and bills of quantities appropriate to the range of contractors likely to be invited to bid, and to the craftsmen and sub-contractors likely to be available. Reference has been made in Chapter 7 to the standards, codes of practice and building regulations to be adopted or conformed to.

Selection of contractors and sub-contractors to bid is crucial, and a full study should be made of local practice, the capability of local contractors and the presence of international contractors. A contractor may already have been appointed by the client (as in Case Study 8 in Tokyo) or be part of the client's consortium (as in Case Study 14 in Moscow). International contractors may already be active and experienced in the country (as in Case Studies 2 in Tanzania, 11 in Aden and 12 in Saudi Arabia). The choice of contractor may be best made from the combination of an international contractor (with the latest management experience) and a local contractor (with knowledge of the local labour market and traditions, and of local craftsmen).

It is essential therefore to set out criteria for selection and only prequalify those contractors or joint ventures who can demonstrate that they can meet them. In some cases you may come under pressure from the client, for private or political reasons, to prequalify contractors who do not satisfy the criteria: this must be resisted vigorously.

(c)   *Stages J–L (Construction)*
During construction the work centre moves to the site office or nearby local office. It is usually essential to have there a senior and experienced representative, who can administer the contract and deal with a multitude of contingencies

which may arise, from actions by the contractor, or the client or from external factors such as political events. This is the most testing, as well as the most professionally rewarding, period of the assignment, both for the senior representative and for the firm.

Good communications and support for your representative are at a premium. Not only will he have the responsibility for administering the contract, but he will also have a wide range of office tasks to carry out, and may have other expatriate staff to look after as well. These responsibilities are described more fully in later chapters.

9

People

It is not *what* you know but *who* you know: a rather hackneyed phrase but an appropriate one with which to begin this important chapter. The selection of people to live overseas is of critical importance.

For many people, going abroad to live and work is a significant and traumatic experience. Age, personal qualities, motivation, health, marital status and attitude of spouse, children and education, are all as important as professional, design or technical skills. Let us take these characteristics in turn.

9.1 Age, Personal Qualities, Motivation

(a) A balance needs to be found between the respect which clients may give to an older and more senior member of staff – in many countries 15 years or more of professional experience may be required for MDA-funded work – and the energy, adaptability and fitness of a younger person.

(b) Personal Qualities
     People living and working overseas should ideally have as many as possible of the following characteristics:

     • Sympathy with the people of the country concerned

- Willingness to learn from the country and treat its people as equals
- Some experience of living overseas
- Wide professional experience
- Technical competence
- Flexibility
- Sense of humour
- Self-sufficiency
- Equability
- Energy.

(c) Motivation
People must really want to work overseas, and not regard it as an inferior option. They must feel that it will offer them personal and professional rewards, and that they have something to offer in return. It is important for them to have an open mind to the culture of the country and to be prepared to respond to local conditions.

9.2 Health

Living in a different culture and climate puts great strain on people's mental and physical health and it is thus very important that they are fit and mentally well balanced and remain so during their tour overseas. They should have a medical check-up before travel and on their return.

(a) Health Brief
Before travel a Health Brief should be obtained from the Medical Advisory Service for Travellers Abroad (MASTA) at the London School of Hygiene and Tropical Medicine which keeps an up-to-date databank of health information world-wide. (See contact address in Appendix D.) Health Briefs come in different degrees of detail, from Quick Health Briefs with recommended immunizations and advice on malaria, to comprehensive Health Briefs containing a complete guide and reference for working or living abroad with a personal immunization schedule for up to four people.

(b)   Accessories to Health
       MASTA can also supply

- Lightweight portable personal water purifier
- Insect repellent
- Mosquito bed net
- AIDS and Hepatitis B transmission prevention pack*
- Dental emergency pack.

* MASTA recommends the carriage of this pack outside Western Europe, the USA, Canada, Japan, Australia, Singapore and Hong Kong. Travellers should not go abroad without knowing their blood group, and the pack has a clear space for this information. This may enable tested blood to be found (for example, from a panel of donors held by many Embassies and High Commissions).

(c)   Food and Drink
       It is suggested that people should, as far as possible, consume local, rather than imported, food and drink. Local produce is fresher, less expensive and better suited to local climatic conditions and life-style. In tropical countries it is usually safer to eat cooked food and avoid salads, and only to drink hot drinks and bottled beverages, when away from home and international hotels.

9.3 Marital Status

It is preferable for an individual member of staff going abroad for a long period to go with his family if he has one. This will, of course, depend on his spouse's career and attitude, and the ages of their children. It is sensible to interview the couple together to ensure that they are both keen, temperamentally suited and prepared to go overseas. If the person is not married he may have a long-term partner and you may have to consider whether such a relationship will be acceptable in the country concerned, where views on marriage may be much stricter than at home.

Some married members of staff opt to go abroad on bachelor status for reasons of their spouse's career or their children's schooling, in which case more frequent holiday air-flights home should be provided. Indeed in some cases RMJM has agreed the equivalent number of flights that would have been needed for the family to travel out to the country and return home, to give additional flights to the team member. However, in general, it is preferable to avoid this kind of bachelor status as it can put the marriage under undue stress. It is worth checking if people have continuing home responsibilities (such as elderly relatives to support) as contingencies may arise where urgent compassionate home leave is needed with consequent costs and disruption to the project.

The Women's Corona Society provides useful information and services in the UK and a network of overseas branches for women travelling abroad including:

- Notes for newcomers to about 100 overseas countries
- One-day courses on living overseas (particularly health and welfare, and adaptation to a different culture)
- Children's escort services
- Overseas branch activities.

See contact address in Appendix D.

9.4 Children and Education

The question of appropriate schooling needs to be considered. For children up to ten or twelve years old there is usually adequate English-language schooling available in the country concerned. Above this age there may be adequate schooling in major cities, but often families opt for the alternative of sending their children to boarding schools in the UK. Indeed many boarding schools which were originally formed to provide education for children of the British Colonial civil service, now rely on providing for children of expatriates working overseas on business.

Availability of local English-language schooling should be checked during exploratory missions. Alternatively, contact can be made with the European Council of International Schools (ECIS). Its members include nearly 300 primary and secondary international schools, and more than 250 institutions of higher education and education-related organizations world-wide, all with English as the language of teaching, or one of the major languages. ECIS publishes Directories of over 1000 international school and tertiary institutions, and Guides to School Evaluation and Accreditation and to Entry to Higher Education Worldwide. See contract address in Appendix D.

9.5 Housing

It is important that suitable residential accommodation (either a house or a flat) fully furnished, equipped and serviced is provided for expatriate staff. In the case of the team leader or firm's representative it will need to be large enough for his family and for him to entertain business guests. It will also normally be used to accommodate visitors from head office in the UK. This has the advantage of being cheaper than a hotel, and offering a more relaxed environment in which partners or directors from the UK can discuss personal or project matters with the member of staff and spouse.

9.6 Team Leader and Representative

Your representative and team leader is a key person, and must be selected with great care. He must be able to deal with the client, Local Associates, consultants and contractors as well as local professional advisers, the bank manager, other members of staff and their families. He must be ready to deal with emergencies. From our experience these have included everything from the outbreak of war in Biafra to the accidental death of a team member in Saudi Arabia described in Case Study 12.

The position can be extremely important in career development. It offers an opportunity for a person to take more responsibility than he would at home, to show leadership, and to make a success of an assignment without the overburden of the home office environment. To the right person it can be an exciting challenge.

Suitable nomenclature and status for the team leader along with considerable delegation of authority are necessary to give confidence in the individual's ability to represent your UK practice effectively, without frequent reference back. Overseas representatives need to be kept fully informed of what is happening in the practice at home and elsewhere overseas, to return regularly to the UK to report on the overseas office, and to hear at first hand how the firm in the UK is progressing.

9.7 Culture Shock

I have mentioned earlier the importance of understanding the culture of the country you are working in. This can affect every aspect of meeting and working with local people. In general, the English reserve goes down better than the American instant familiarity and exchange of first names which marks all private and business relationships. The way people greet each other, the way meetings are conducted, dress, respect, punctuality, ways of eating, sense of humour; all need careful attention if you are to get on smoothly in the country concerned. The subject has been well covered for the countries of the EC in John Mole's *Mind Your Manners*[28], which attempts to answer the question "What do I need to know about colleagues from EC countries that will help us work successfully together?" For an understanding of Chinese, Malay and Indian communities in South-east Asia, I recommend *Culture Shock* by JoAnn Craig[28], and a similar book for Thailand.

A useful series of courses which can help staff prepare for and adjust to the culture of the country they will work in are run by the Centre for International Briefing, Farnham Castle, covering:

- Familiarization with politics, economy and working environment
- Local business practices, personal values, attitudes and culture
- Local perception of expatriates
- Avoiding causing personal or professional offence
- Coping with the new environment
- Gaining respect and confidence of local people
- Expatriate living conditions (schools, health, leisure, etc.).

Consultants recruited for long-term assignments by ODA are encouraged to attend these courses at Farnham Castle.

9.8 Cultural Disorientation

In *Culture Shock* JoAnn Craig describes how the combination of physical differences (such as climate, food, health, hygiene, fatigue), environmental differences (such as housing, roads, shops, produce, money) and cultural differences (such as etiquette, traditions, language, non-verbal communications) can cause cultural disorientation. This can lead people to behave like one of three basic types of person:

- The *encapsulator*, who withdraws into a bubble, haunts the expatriate club, and has minimum contact with local people.
- The *cosmopolitan*, who has a foot in both camps, and adjusts to both the expatriate society and local society.
- The *absconder*, who goes "native", falls in love with the local life-style, and may marry a local person and take local citizenship.

Of these, the *cosmopolitan* is the most likely to be successful, both personally and in carrying out the assignment, particularly if supported by his family. The others may well develop personal problems, excessive drinking, marital infidelity or some of the other characteristics so well described by Somerset Maugham in his short stories from Malaya and Borneo[29]. Such people cannot be wholly effective working overseas.

9.9 Social Life

As can be seen from the preceding sections, social life is of great importance abroad, for the family, for relaxation, for meeting other expatriates, and in participation in the local community. There will generally be a club for expatriates and local people, and sporting clubs with similar membership (e.g. for golf, sailing or polo). Membership of such clubs is a quick way to get to know people locally and to become integrated into the country's way of life. RMJM regards it as essential for all expatriate staff to belong to one or more such clubs of their choice, and usually pays for a family subscription to one club for each person resident overseas.

9.10 Pay

We add a percentage to UK salaries to take account of:

- Separation from the UK
- Local hardship (due to climate, living conditions, etc.)
- Local cost of living
- Additional responsibility (of team leader or representative).

The figure has varied from 10% in Malaysia to 80% in Nigeria.
    A useful advisory service is provided by Economic Conditions Abroad Ltd (ECA) covering:

- Salary trends in the country
- Benefits (including accommodation, school fees, pensions, cars, medical insurance, leave and club subscriptions)
- Tax
- Remittance
- Cost of living indices
- Legal requirements
- Social security benefits
- Devaluation and inflation.

The service requires you to keep ECA informed of your staff's pay and benefits, and their participation in annual cost-of-living questionnaires.
    In addition, Business International can provide detailed information on executive living costs world-wide including housing, household goods, utilities, clothing, domestic help, recreation and entertainment, local transport, hotels and restaurants, education and health care.
    For contact addresses see Appendix D.

9.11 Contract

The scope and headings of staff contracts are described in Chapter 13.

9.12 Return to the UK

As time goes on the question of re-entry to professional work in the UK assumes more and more prominence in the mind of the overseas member of staff. It is important that he is not forgotten in the firm's forward plans for deployment of staff on future projects. The partner or director in charge of the overseas project must be active both in ensuring that this happens and in keeping the person overseas fully aware of developments and prospects at home.

10
Office Administration

10.1 Local Administration

In order to keep technical staff productively engaged on project work and avoid being distracted by practical problems of everyday life, good local administration will need to deal with aspects which go beyond what is normal in the UK. These may include:

(a) Staff housing
Arranging leases, connections and paying utilities, emergency repairs, maintenance, day and night watchmen, and insurance.

(b) Schools for children
Identifying local schools, paying fees, and arranging transport.

(c) Medical and dental care
Finding and arranging for routine and emergency health care and insurance.

(d) Registration with the local British Embassy, High Commission or Consulate in case of emergency.

(e) Immigration procedures
Arranging for visas to be issued and renewed.

(f)   Employment permits
Arranging and renewing permits.

(g)   Cars
Arranging purchase or leasing, servicing, drivers and insurance.

(h)   Security
Office watchmen, and avoidance of risks of kidnap.

In addition, the local office will need to replicate in some degree all of the administrative activities of head office.

10.2 Head Office Support

Strong support is needed from head office to match many of the following administrative activities:

(a)   Arranging travel and insurance for people and their families going overseas on long-term assignments, children returning to school, and for people going out for short visits.

(b)   Sending out emergency personal supplies not obtainable overseas.

(c)   Sending out books, technical information, and drawing office supplies not available locally abroad.

(d)   Obtaining visas.

(e)   Making arrangements in cases of emergency repatriation, illness, or compassionate leave.

(f)   Providing general news from the home office. This is important for local morale and to ensure that people overseas do not feel forgotten.

(g)   Arranging substitute staff by maintaining CVs of back-up staff available in an emergency or to cover periods when people overseas are on leave. I have already pointed out that clients overseas are reluctant to accept substitutes, so this needs as much advance preparation as possible. In some cases it may not be necessary to provide cover for leave, for example when local deputies can stand in. However, the period may be long enough to justify alternative members of staff travelling out with enough overlap to take over and hand back responsibilities. In cases of repatriation or serious illness it may be necessary to obtain agreement from both the funding client and the user client to a substitute, with a new negotiated charging rate.

(h) Maintaining insurance cover. As an employer you are responsible under the Health and Safety at Work, etc. Act 1974 for employees' health, safety and welfare at work, even if the place of work is overseas, although this may depend upon a recent ruling in the Court of Appeal on the number of employees and length of time spent overseas. You should inform your insurance company of employees working overseas, so that the employer's liability insurance which you must maintain by law is extended to cover them. As noted in Section 6.5, you will also need to extend your Professional Indemnity policy to cover work overseas.

10.3 Language

Confucius said "If language is not correct then what is written is not what is meant; if what is written is not what is meant then what ought to be done remains undone." Although English is one of the major commercial languages understood world-wide, lack of command of a local language can be a grave disadvantage.

A useful distinction to make is between *interpretation* and *translation*. RMJM's design for the UNESCAP Conference Centre in Bangkok (Case Study 6) has to provide for both:

• Interpreters provide a continuous interpretation into six official languages of what a speaker is saying, conveying *verbally* as far as possible the character and sense of what is said.
• Translation is the *written* transcript of statements, minutes and other papers into one of the six official languages, aiming as far as possible to be factually accurate.

(a) Interpretation
For most senior people and representatives it is the *interpretation* of what is said, and the ability to communicate *verbally* in a foreign language which is important:

- It is essential to sell one's services and experience in the language of the client.
- It is more polite and culturally acceptable to speak the client's language, even if badly. Even a few words or phrases can make all the difference to the outcome of a presentation or negotiation, or the smooth running of a project.

Among the plethora of language courses and advisory centres for people wanting to learn foreign languages, the following can provide a useful starting point:

- The Institute of Linguists advises on language training and maintains a register of interpreters and translators.
- OMTRAC offers an advisory service on training programmes.
- Farnham Castle runs regular intensive week-long tuition courses in French, German, Spanish, Arabic, Bahasa Malay/Indonesian and Japanese, and occasional courses in other languages.
- The Association of Language-Export Centres is a network of 23 L-X centres covering most of England, Scotland and Wales and providing:
  - assessment of language training needs
  - language training for business
  - interpreting and translation
  - country, cultural and trade briefings.

For contact addresses see Appendix D.

From a survey carried out by the OMTRAC Language Advisory and Referral Service covering 50 companies (including some providing professional services), most agreed that total immersion or intensive courses provide the quickest and most effective method of learning a language. From a cross-section of 575 requests for advice received between 1988 and 1989, three-quarters were for the principal European languages.

OMTRAC estimates that it takes at least 150 hours for somebody to acquire basic competence from scratch, and at least 600 hours to become fluent (depending on which language and the educational background of the individual). Typical charges are:

- Intensive (35–40 hours per week)   £750–£1150
- Individual (one-to-one) per hour   £20–£35
- Interpreting per hour   £20–£45

(b) Translation

It is vital that legal documents, reports, specifications and accounts are accurately translated into the language of the country concerned. This can be done by bilingual secretaries, technical translators or specialized translation agencies. It is usually best to choose people who are translating into their native language. The accurate translation of technical phrases is extremely important to avoid any misunder-standing, whether with the client, local authorities, Local Associates or the construction team. OMTRAC estimates the cost of translation services as £50–£100 per 1000 words. Accounts will need to be translated into local languages in some countries before audit can take place (for example, in Saudi Arabia and Thailand). As already mentioned, the Institute of Linguists has a register of translators. Technical Help to Exporters provides a Translations Section which can be of great assistance in ensuring that specialist terminology is accurately translated. De Pinna Scorers and John Venn have legal and commercial translators from and into the main European languages. For contact addresses see Appendix D.

(c) A general glossary of technical terms for work in Europe may be found in a *Dictionary of Building Terms* in twelve languages published in Moscow: in Bulgarian, Czech, English, French, German, Hungarian, Mongolian, Polish, Romanian, Russian and Serbo-Croat[30].

10.4 Communications

(a) Good communications between head office and the local office are essential, with awareness of the windows created by different time zones and contact points out of office hours at either end. Sometimes the time difference works productively. For example, when negotiating a contract in Manila (GMT+8) I could telex a number of queries to

London at the end of one day, receive the answers before breakfast, and have the negotiating papers reprocessed during breakfast ready for the start of the next day's negotiations: and Sir Norman Foster & Partners effectively worked a 21-hour day taking advantage of the 9-hour difference between London and Tokyo (Case Study 8).

(b)   Modes

All modes of communications have their uses, but may require some research and discipline to be used effectively and economically:

- Cable
- Telephone
- Telex
- Facsimile
- Electronic mail
- Accompanied baggage
- Courier
- Post.

Compatibility of computer programs and disks should be studied, and care taken to ensure speedy customs clearance of drawings and models (by providing windows in packaging).

(c)   Personal

Local morale is greatly enhanced by regularly sending out personal mail, professional magazines, newspapers, periodicals and videos.

11
Finance

After people, the second major constraint on working overseas is finance. This chapter is not intended as an exhaustive exposition of the subject, but rather an introduction to aspects on which you will need professional advice.

As you will have observed, the range of contingencies to be faced in working overseas is very large. The risks involved must be listed and quantified at the outset, and regularly examined and updated as the project proceeds. The risk management implicit in this process is essential to the eventual profitability of the project.

11.1 Financial Information

A clear view of finances is a fundamental need when exporting, with strong management systems and controls. Techniques need to be developed for surviving liquidity problems arising from longer credit periods, political risks, currency variations, harsher taxation regimes and proliferating documentation. Financial and legal information is needed not only by the home office management for policy-making and control but also by prospective clients, funding agencies and banks or institutions lending funds, both at home and overseas. Hence the firm's personal, financial and management track record must be well documented.

Management techniques are required for dealing with a multiplicity of banks, accountants, lawyers, other expert advisers (e.g. insurance brokers) and perhaps a mixture of partnerships, companies, branches and offices in different locations. For the balance sheet, the usual bankers' touchstones loom even larger as projects enter areas of greater risk and uncertainty and become more difficult to control. The equity base/capital gearing is critical, as few banks want to put more into a firm than the owners themselves are prepared to risk. Security or collateral for borrowing needs to be first class and interest cover needs to be sufficient to repay funds and meet interest charges. Tax affairs need to be up to date.

For financial planning and the requirements of banks, clarity is needed on the amount, purpose and timing of finance required and the financial position and prospects of the firm. You need to show that you can apply and manage funds effectively.

Audited accounts should be analysed for profitability by geographic areas over a five-year period. The balance sheet needs to be carefully analysed and annotated, with trading and cash flow projected for a reasonable period ahead, certainly for the length of the next project being undertaken. Assumptions need to be realistic and clearly stated. Lenders impose conditions that have professional as well as financial implications, e.g. the danger of loss of independence, of overtrading (of people, money or time) or undercapitalization. Before making a project submission, the costing and reimbursement methods, financial sequences, cash flow and banking or other financial support available (including export insurance) need to be worked out carefully.

11.2 Banking

The key is to find a banker willing to lend against overseas fees debtors; there are plenty of funds available, but these are dependent on satisfying the criteria for lending. The banker asks about bonds (such as bid bonds, performance bonds, guarantees against advance payments) for clients or for overseas bankers as a counter-indemnity, about the overdrafts needed overseas, and any guarantees in that connection. The banker may ask for a confirmed, irrevocable letter of credit from the client. He may look critically at facilities with other bankers for particular areas or projects. Some banks overseas are nationalized and not permitted to grant overdraft facilities. Only the firm is able to coordinate relationships and facilities with the various banks used.

11.3 Accounting

Accounting, auditing and bookkeeping methods, project costing, budgeting, monitoring and financial statements (including frequency and detail); and integration into a home or world-wide system are all affected by where the project team is set up, whether at home, in an overseas office, or on site, and whether by itself or with other teams.

Accountants are needed at home who know about exporting, the tax reliefs available, techniques for dealing with exchange variations and so on. Accountants overseas are needed who have knowledge of local tax for expatriate staff, custom duties, remittance laws, and tax-clearance procedures. It helps if they have links with your home firm. They should advise on what audit methods are acceptable locally, and whether the audit of time, costs, and overheads are acceptable to the overseas regime. Accounting timetables need to be adjusted to maintain a grip on the firm as a whole, a branch, a joint venture, or a project. Partners or directors, bankers, home tax authorities, and insurers all need up-to-date financial information. Advice is needed from the tax-planning consultant on dual residence and the anti-avoidance sections of relevant legislation.

11.4 Exchange Control

Advice may be needed on home exchange control regulations, such as consent to open an account overseas, to receive or spend foreign currency, to make payments to non-residents, to incorporate overseas or establish a non-resident subsidiary, to own property overseas, and to grant guarantees in favour of non-residents. Procedures are carried out either by the home bank or, if applicable, by direct application to the national central bank of the country in which the project is located. Advice on overseas exchange control regulations is needed from local accountants and lawyers.

11.5 Export Credits Guarantee Department

A critical element to consider is the insurance of getting paid overseas, and being able to remit funds to the UK. The most effective way of doing this is through the Export Credits Guarantee Department (ECGD) although it is also possible in some cases to insure in the market.

Among the wide range of facilities offered by ECGD there are two of particular importance to you when working overseas.

(a) Insurance against the risk of your client overseas failing to make payment as properly due under your agreement. ECGD normally offers up to 90% cover against commercial risk (i.e. simple commercial failure of the client to pay) and up to 95% cover against country risk (i.e. failure of payment through a local factor such as blocking of foreign exchange transactions or outbreak of war). You would normally take out insurance on a project-by-project basis (under a Specific Services Guarantee), but if you have a repetitive pattern of short-term work in several markets you may take out a Comprehensive Services Guarantee. You should apply in the first instance to ECGD (see Appendix D), who will advise on the most appropriate policy. The short-term business is being hived off into a separate Insurance Services Group, as a subsidiary of the Dutch insurance company NCM, operating in Cardiff.

(b) In certain cases, it is possible to arrange an ECGD guarantee for a UK bank loan for the financing of your services to an overseas client. Clearly the securing of such an ECGD guarantee facilitates the arrangement of financing for markets that the commercial banks might otherwise decline. Additionally, and most importantly, for certain less-developed countries ECGD is able to support the banks in offering finance at interest rates and on repayment conditions that are softer than normal commercial terms. Applications for such financing assistance are usually made by first approaching one of the commercial banks who will then assist in forwarding applications to ECGD and in the preparation of suitable draft loan agreements.

It is important therefore to contact ECGD at the earliest stage to discuss ECGD's view of a particular country or project, for these reasons:

- ECGD cover is not available for all overseas markets and in others is subject to country limits on the volume of exposure that ECGD is able to accept at any time.
- The negotiation of loan terms to the satisfaction of all parties, often involving the agreement of a sovereign guarantee by the client's government, can be a lengthy business.
- ECGD guarantees can involve you in substantial premiums payable in advance.

You can cover not only the work of your firm in the UK but also, under the Investment Insurance Scheme, the work of any overseas subsidiaries, or your share in a joint venture. The EC is not regarded as a domestic market, and work there can continue to be covered after 1992. Basically, you will be quoted a premium for each project at the outset which will hold firm for the whole period of its execution.

If ECGD cover is not available for a country or project you would be unwise to proceed unless you were certain of being paid outside the country in hard currency freely transferable to the UK. Equally, there may be countries or clients sufficiently gilt-edged that it is not worth the cost of taking out ECGD cover. You should also note that changes in exchange rates can adversely affect the value of fees due when claimed under ECGD policies.

11.6 Project Related Finance

You will probably need to prepare a careful business plan to convince your home bank manager to agree a facility for the preliminary stages until the project is secured and fees start to flow.

(a)   Business Development
The cost of business development can be considerable, and is an investment which may take some time to recoup. At each stage as much as possible should be done at home, with maximum preparation to make the more expensive visits overseas cost-effective. Advantage should be taken of UK government financial support, for example in joining overseas missions.

(b)   Winning the project
There are three aspects which need careful assessment once a prospective project has been identified:

- The investment in preparing the technical submission (and design submission if needed). Although other factors may determine where this work is done, your costs will be a major consideration.
- As already indicated in Section 5.5, the Financial Submission must be finely judged:
  - to be a winning figure
  - to provide a flexible basis for negotiation, and running the project.

  A considerable amount of information will be needed to prepare the submission, and tailor it to the right format.
- Negotiation to agree a mutually acceptable basis for charging fees and expenses which recovers the investment so far, and provides a profitable operation and outcome.

(c)   Setting Up
It is likely that considerable initial funds will be needed to set up a local office, obtain housing, furniture, equipment, and vehicles, hire local staff, and mobilize the team. All this needs to be taken into account in the cash flow prediction

for the project, with advance payments made by the client. The client will probably need an advance payment guarantee from a local bank (payable on call).

At this stage all the operating procedures for a local office need to be set up similar to those you have in the UK, including:

- Opening bank accounts
- Cheque signatories
- Petty cash procedures
- Payroll procedures
- Bookkeeping
- Submission of fee and expenses invoices
- Payment of rents, utilities and other costs.

(d) Implementation
   During this stage careful monitoring of cash flow, project costs, bank statements etc. will be needed.

12
Taxation and Law

I cannot in this book do more than draw attention to the importance of taxation and legal aspects of working overseas.

12.1 Taxation

You will need tax planning advice on the effect of tax on the legal trading entity used, where the work is done, accounting methods and timetables, profitability, and cash flow. The more countries you operate in, the more complex the position becomes, especially for partnerships, because of the interaction of the timing of capital allowances, advance payments subject to varying exchange rates, withholding taxes, double/unilateral tax relief and exchange control, incidence and timing. To solve these equations with more than a few variables requires a computer. Speedily produced accounts leading to prompt tax filing overseas have a direct effect on cash flow at final account stage, release of bonds, and remittances to the home office. The way different authorities view trading figures is vital because sometimes they ignore losses and impose a tax on, say, a notional or deemed profit, related to turnover. No relief against tax may be given for tax paid overseas on a loss as defined by the home tax authorities. The various ways in which the same information is presented to different authorities, how exchange gains or losses are dealt with and how home indirect overheads are allocated to various projects and branches are key subjects involving the design and workings of the home office costing system.

It is advisable as well to understand clearly the home and overseas tax effects on short- and long-term contracts, direct pay, and other emoluments and allowances (spouses' fares, school fees and so on). Taxation considerations radically change first thoughts when it comes to a partner residing overseas, leading perhaps to the setting up of an overseas partnership that can also yield relief for its partners at home. Overall return and control over financial affairs is more important than minimizing the tax paid.

In particular, you will find that working overseas involves you in the tax affairs of individual members of staff as well as those of your firm. For example, in some countries you may pay individuals partly off-shore without their paying local tax, and thus produce a more advantageous cash flow and better margin on a project.

12.2 Legal Matters

Hand in hand with advice on taxation you will need good legal advice, both on legal entities to be created, and on individual projects.

(a)   Families of legal systems
It is important to recognise the different families of legal systems and customs applicable overseas:

- Common law systems (mainly in the UK, the USA and their countries of influence) are based on case law, although there are considerable local differences (for example, between England and Scotland, and between Federal and State systems in the USA).
- Romano-Germanic family based on Roman law (mainly in France and other continental European countries and their countries of influence). The rule of law is conceived as a rule of conduct intimately linked to ideas of justice

and morality, formulated separately from its administration and practical application in the courts.

- Family of socialist laws (in the CIS, China and countries of influence) based on Marxism–Leninism, and strictly subordinated to prevailing economic conditions. Contracts are only to assure execution of the current economic plan, not to make a profit.
- Philosophical or religious systems (in Muslim countries, Israel and India). The emphasis is on individual duties derived from religious rules concerning human relationships. In Muslim countries these are based on the *Koran*, subsequent scholastic interpretations, and juristic reasoning by analogy. In India these were incorporated into common law under the period of British influence.
- Traditional or customary laws (e.g. in sub-Saharan Africa) with an overlay of relevant common law or Romano-Germanic laws laid down under Western influence.

The implications for companies and individuals vary widely. For example, the Napoleonic code may demand physical retribution for professional negligence. The Islamic strict liability code may impose 10 to 20 years of legal liability, sometimes jointly with all others involved. In the United States, exemplary and punitive damages are a criminal award which cannot be insured against, unlike their equivalent, aggravated damages, in the United Kingdom. The development and characteristics of different legal systems are described in detail in David and Brierley's *Major Legal Systems*[31].

Needless to say, the laws in the CIS and countries of influence are in a state of flux, following *perestroika* and the declarations of independent states, on which specialist legal advice should be sought.

(b) Resolution of conflicts

You will also need to recognize the potential conflicts arising from these different systems, and the means of resolving these conflicts. For example:

- The governing law for various contracts and agreements may differ (for example, between your agreement with your client, and the contract between your client and the contractor), and the applicable law in cases of dispute may need to be stated.

- Your rights to enforce a judgment against someone under foreign jurisdiction may need investigation.
- The jurisdiction of courts in the country of building and in the different country of domicile, say, of a co-consultant, or contractor, may differ.
- Insurance cover applicable in different countries may need to be coordinated.
- Definitions of your duties may differ in the governing laws for different countries.

For a fuller discussion of these aspects see the chapter on international work by architects in the *Architect's Legal Handbook*[32]. This also gives a useful introduction to the architect's responsibilities in the different countries of the EC and the USA.

(c)   Aspects to be considered

Your legal adviser may need to consider many inter-related financial, technical and administrative matters. He will advise on the operation and requirements of local laws, codes, and customs, including immigration, labour and insurance. Commercial and professional registration involving complex documents and long lead times may be needed. The simplest, most tax-effective legal entity should be chosen for practising. The costs of setting up and maintaining different entities vary greatly, as do their tax holiday effects. Local Associates and sponsors may be involved, either at arm's length or as participants. A decision about whether to form a partnership, a joint venture, or a consortium must be made while respecting indigenization laws stipulating the degree of local participation and the commission or share payable. Owning or leasing property may be dependent on special local prohibitions or conditions. A notarized power of attorney will be needed for your senior representative. Apart from notarized deeds and accounts of the firm and professional qualifications to prepare, there is the primary agreement with the client to draw up; consultancy agreements to make with other firms in the team and local consultants; and interfirm, joint venture or consortium agreements to make as already described in earlier chapters.

Fundamentally, the objective of all these agreements is the mutual understanding by the partners of the meaning of the wording of the agreements, together with legal enforceability. All agreements will need to spell out the duties and tasks to be carried out by the parties; the inputs and outputs required; the timetables for them; methods for calculating remuneration; consequences of delay; how, when and where disputes will be resolved, and applicable laws.

(d)   EEIGs

An interesting possibility for setting up a legal entity across the boundaries of the EC exists in the form of European Economic Interest Groupings (EEIGs). These provide a flexible method of organizing a multinational group to seek or carry out one or more projects, in one or more EC countries, without full-scale integration. RMJM is the British member of an EEIG, Designers International, registered in London, covering most countries in the EC and EFTA. The main characteristics of an EEIG are:

- It is a separate legal entity which can undertake contracts.
- It is non-profit making and thus not a separate accounting or taxable entity. Any profits from its activities are shared by its members.
- It must have at least two members from different countries.
- It must have an official address and be registered in the country where the main activity is located.
- The applicable law is that of the country where it is registered.
- Its members have joint and several liabilities for its debts.

Copies of EEIG Registration Forms are obtainable from the RIBA, and the UK Registry is located at the London office of the Commission of the European Communities. See contact address in Appendix D.

12.3 Advisers

You must therefore take advice from international firms of accountants and lawyers in the UK, and from local accountants and lawyers in each country (or even a state within a country) in which you plan to work. In some countries taxation and legal advice may be available from one firm, as in Thailand (Case Study 6).

Advice on firms of solicitors in the UK specializing in different countries is available from the Legal Practice Directorate (International) of the Law Society. Most large firms of solicitors in London have departments specializing in geographical areas and publish briefing notes on setting up a business in specific countries. Similarly, large firms of accountants issue briefing notes on taxation in specific countries.

Advice on Notaries Public can be obtained through your solicitors. The largest firm in London, De Pinna Scorers and John Venn, also offers a service of legal and commercial translation from and into the main European languages. For contact address see Appendix D.

13

Implications for Individual Architects Working Overseas

Hitherto, this book has been addressed to firms of architects practising overseas or wishing to do so. I now turn to the position of the individual architect who is either sent overseas to work for his firm or who wishes to go overseas on his own account for employment by a local practice or by another expatriate firm.

The earlier chapters of this book will all have relevance to the individual who wishes to work overseas, particularly Chapter 9 on People. However, it is worth looking again at aspects arising from other chapters, from the viewpoint of an individual.

13.1 Opportunities in Different Countries

The opportunities in the different categories in Chapter 1 are different for you from those for firms of architects. The developed world is generally well provided with local architects, and will tend to use them in preference to foreign architects, despite the lowering of barriers to professional practice (e.g. in the EC). The developing world and oil-rich countries have fewer architects but are tending towards indigenization of architectural practice (as, for example, in Nigeria). There are opportunities in such cases for experienced architects to work as partners or senior associates in local firms. You would then also be well placed to promote or respond to the formation later of joint associations with firms of architects from the English-speaking developed world. There are also opportunities for work in senior positions in the public sector, which are advertised from time to time in the UK.

The number of architects per head of population varies considerably. In Italy, for example, there is about one architect per 1000 (and as many students again), while in Holland there is about one per 6000 and in Indonesia nearer one per 100 000 population, in comparison with about one per 2000 in the UK.

While the Middle East was the developing market of the 1970s (and may be so again if the price of oil goes up substantially) most eyes are now on the EC, South-east Asia and the Pacific Rim, as they are likely to become the leading development areas of the 1990s. You may well want to consider the effect of *perestroika* in the CIS and Eastern Europe, where considerable investment in development is likely to be made by the West, as soon as there are realistic prospects of political stability.

Some measure of the possibilities of work abroad can be seen from the number of RIBA members overseas. Over 5000 members (about 20% of the total) live and work abroad, mainly in developed Commonwealth countries, South Africa and the USA, with a small number (barely 2% of members) living in the EC. These figures can, of course, only give a partial picture as they include foreign architects, and exclude architects who are not RIBA members.

13.2 Professional Qualifications

A British professional qualification is generally accepted overseas (although not currently in the USA). Within the EC any architect with a recognized professional qualification should be able to register for practice in any other country in the EC, under the Architects Directive 1985. However, its implementation is rather uneven. While most EC countries had legislation complete in 1992, some, such as Belgium and Spain, had only implemented the Directive selectively and Greece had still to start. It is due to be extended to EFTA countries early in 1993.

Every country has different requirements, so you would be

wise to consult the RIBA, which maintains a dossier for the latest situation in most countries in the world. In many countries it is necessary to pass an examination in local regulations before being able to practise fully, make submissions to local authorities and approve drawings (for example, to become an "Approved Person" in Hong Kong).

13.3 Constraints

There are a number of constraints to working overseas which will apply in most cases and which you will need to overcome, including entry visas (which may only be available if a promise of employment has already been obtained), residential visas and work permits (which may, for example in Australia, be issued for only one year), and any laws affecting the employment and freedom of movement for women (in Muslim countries). You should check rates of pay (for example, in Italy they barely cover the cost of rent) as well as the rules for remittance of earnings to the UK, rates of local taxation, and withholding taxes.

Finding a job locally may not be easy as there are often no professional employment agencies, and no weekly professional journals. Thus personal approaches are important, and you should take an easily portable portfolio and references with you.

While knowledge of English is a useful asset, it will be a great advantage to speak and write the local language reasonably fluently in countries where English is not the principal language of business.

13.4 Families

If you have a family you will no doubt want to take them with you overseas and an important distinction is likely to arise between the developed world and elsewhere. This is that you are unlikely to receive assistance from your employer towards housing, schooling, clubs, and so on in *developed* countries, although you will probably do so elsewhere. This will obviously be important when you consider the pay which you are seeking.

Social life is important in relation to both other expatriates and the local community. People need opportunities for relaxation and sport to get away from office colleagues out of working hours. Much of your family happiness will depend on your spouse's personal qualities and ability to adapt to an unfamiliar environment and culture. In tropical countries, heat and humidity require a high degree of adaptability and tolerance. Special care is needed in respect of local customs, e.g. consumption of alcohol, dress, physical gestures, and the segregation of women. If you wish your children to accompany you abroad, you should check the quality and availability of appropriate schools, and whether places are available in them.

13.5 Standing of Employer

You would do well to check the standing and bona fides of your prospective employer if he is unknown or unfamiliar to you. This may be done by reference to the local equivalent of the RIBA or ARCUK, the local/British Chamber of Commerce, or Dun & Bradstreet's Business Information Service, whichever is most appropriate.

13.6 Taxation

You will naturally have to pay tax either at home or overseas, depending on the timing and extent of your overseas residence, and any return periods to the UK for business or holidays. If your permanent home is in the UK (i.e. you are domiciled here) to be exempt from UK tax you have to be resident abroad for more than a complete fiscal year, with complicated limits on how long you may visit the UK on business or for holidays. If you are employed abroad for at least a year (but not covering a fiscal year) you will not be liable for your overseas earnings, but will be liable for tax on unearned income at home (e.g. property rental) and capital gains. The amount you are due to pay will depend on the rules in the UK or foreign country which apply, and whether there is a Double Taxation Relief Agreement between the UK and the country concerned.

You (and your spouse) will need to take professional advice on tax to establish the most favourable way of managing where and how your income is paid, and to optimize when you travel out and return to the UK. The *Daily Telegraph Guide to Working Abroad*[33] contains a helpful chapter on this subject.

13.7 Personal Implications

The *Daily Telegraph Guide* also gives useful references to all the personal implications of working overseas. This includes advice on:

• Financial planning
• National insurance
• Medical insurance
• Your house
• Your children's education
• Surveys of 35 major countries.

13.8 Alternatives

An alternative to seeking employment overseas as an individual is to work for a British consultancy firm, which will take responsibility for dealing with most of the practical aspects. Reference should be made to the RIBA's *International Directory*, and to the *Members Directory* of the British Consultants Bureau, to identify suitable firms to which to apply.

There are other ways to find employment overseas: for example, by registering with agencies which recruit individuals for specific assignments, such as the World Bank, the ODA, VSO and REDR (Registered Engineers for Disaster Relief, which despite its title includes other professional disciplines). In all these cases prior experience of work in developing countries is an essential qualification.

13.9 When to go

There seem to be three optimum times in an architectural career to work abroad:

- As a student, when a year abroad (particularly in a developed country) may be counted towards the necessary practical experience leading to qualification. Although you may find it personally fulfilling to work in developing countries as a student, you must recognize that you will only be of limited use to them.
- As a young architect with five years of professional experience.
- As a mature architect with over 20 years of practice, when any children are grown up and self-supporting.

You may decide that the attractions of life and professional practice abroad are so great that you want to emigrate permanently. However, if you decide not to do so, you should plan for your return to the UK and maintain contacts here in preparation for resuming your professional career, with as much care as you have taken in planning to work abroad. In any case, you will find that working overseas will enhance your professional experience and provide a valuable international perspective to your career, which will be of particular interest to firms with an international orientation.

13.10 Contract

You should take special care with your contract since it will need to cover so many contingencies which do not apply in a UK contract. These will need all the more careful examination in developing and oil-rich countries where the employer may not be used to employing expatriates, or know the life-style to which they are accustomed. A checklist of factors which need to be considered for inclusion in the contract, based on the list in the RIBA *Practice and Management Handbook* 1981, is set out in Appendix B. A fuller checklist is included in Chapter 11 of the *Daily Telegraph Guide*[33].

13.11 Some Practical Suggestions before Departure

From experience I suggest the following precautions before leaving for a developing country:

- Take the means to pay for excess baggage at the airport (e.g. miscellaneous charges order) and for hotels in transit and on arrival (credit cards).
- Arrange for your employer to meet you on arrival, and have his office and home telephone numbers in case of mishap or delay.
- Take a letter confirming employment, notarized if necessary, and an open return ticket.
- Take separate photocopies of key pages of your passport, including any visa, and of your certificate of inoculations in case they are lost or stolen. Mine were taken at gunpoint in Nigeria en route to the airport, and took over a week to replace!
- Take separate photocopies of your travellers cheques, credit cards and driving licence, and insure against loss.
- Take some American dollars in cash, which are almost universally accepted for taxis and tips, for use in transit.
- Get any medical or dental work done before you leave, and take a copy of the prescription if you wear spectacles.
- Take a notarized copy of your professional and birth certificates.

14
Conclusion

If you have read thus far you will have some idea of the ways in which designing buildings and contract administration overseas differ from the same activities in the UK. You will therefore be aware of the risks you may run in working overseas, which you will need to assess before making any commitment. The illustrative Case Studies give examples of some of these risks in practice, although in any one case only a small number apply.

Nigel Mansfield has summed up the benefits and disadvantages of overseas work for consulting engineers which could equally well apply to RMJM's experience as architects[34]:

Benefits	Disadvantages
Firm's standards improved	Heavy front-end investments
Greater technical competence achieved	Large overheads
Job satisfaction for staff	Currency exchange complications
Prestige for firm	Higher margins necessary
Useful staff kept employed	High-risk business
Financial turnover increased	Client misunderstands nature of service offered
Projects obtained of larger size and longer duration	Wear and tear on individual senior staff
Balancing effect on overall workload	Hard to find right calibre of staff
Greater opportunity and profitability	Free for all on fees

A number of general principles emerge:

- Much more time needs to be spent in management and administration of jobs overseas than at home, particularly on office and domestic overheads, and dealing with personal problems of staff.
- The selection of the right people to go and work overseas is vital to the success of the enterprise.
- The control of finance is crucially important, from preliminary risk assessment and making the initial submission, through advance fee payments to payment of tax and the receipt of final fees.
- Professional advice from lawyers, accountants and insurance brokers, at home and overseas, is essential to success.
- An understanding of the culture and strategic objectives of the country concerned is central to appropriate design and happy working relationships.
- However much expatriate architects are needed in developing countries there is a great deal of suspicion and resistance to be overcome and one measure of success will be how far this has been achieved.

Working overseas is not for the faint-hearted or the opportunist: but with humility, skill and dedication the results can be very rewarding, whether in the form of great works of architecture or solutions to some of the world's problems of shelter and space for human activity, or in making a reasonable profit. Individuals can benefit too in personal achievement and development away from the bureaucracy of the UK, and in building up savings.

At this moment in our history, Britain needs to export to survive, and one of our most valuable commodities is the skill of our architects. If this book can help show how this so-called invisible export can be developed it will have achieved its purpose.

Case Study 1: Castle Peak Power Stations, Hong Kong

Design and contract administration of control and administration blocks and architectural advice on Power Stations A and B (1640 MW and 2710 MW respectively).

Location: New Territories, Hong Kong
Client: A-Station: Kowloon Electricity Supply Co.
B-Station: Castle Peak Power Station Co.
Both owned: EXXON 60%
China Light and Power Company (CLP) 40%
Value: £400 million
Dates: Appointed 1978
Completion A-Station 1984
B-Station 1989

Team

L G Mouchel & Partners and L G Mouchel & Partners (Asia): Civil Engineers & Quantity Surveyors
RMJM & Partners (Hong Kong): Architects, Landscape Architects
J Roger Preston: Building Services (A-Station)
Kennedy & Donkin International: Building Services (B-Station)
Brian Clouston & Partners: Landscape Architects

Business development

RMJM were invited as architects by CLP partly through contacts on the Central Electricity Generating Board (who had been seconded to CLP and subsequently stayed on), experience of designing power stations in Scotland, and through working on projects in Hong Kong since 1965. CLP had formed joint venture companies with EXXON of USA to own the power stations, with CLP taking responsibility for project management and operations. A comprehensive plant design and supply contract was negotiated with GEC Turbine Generators (UK) for the A-Station with Mouchel as Civil Engineers to whom RMJM were sub-consultants. For the B-Station Mouchel were appointed directly by CLP with RMJM again as sub-consultants to Mouchel. The civil construction and the erection and commissioning of the plant supplied by GEC were arranged separately by CLP.

Setting up

The practice of architecture in the Crown Colony is regulated by the Hong Kong Institute of Architects and the Architects Registration Board on similar lines to the RIBA and ARCUK in the UK. All private sector projects are subject to the Hong Kong Government's Building Regulations. Public buildings are exempt. Projects have to be carried out under the control of Authorized Persons (APs) who have passed an interview and have had appropriate experience in Hong Kong in the application of local planning procedures and building regulations. The regulation requires the appointment of an AP to take individual responsibility for the satisfactory design of any project and its compliance with the Building Regulations. All drawings have to be signed by APs who are thereafter responsible for any building failures. See Case Study 15 for more detail.

Appropriate design and technology

The climate is tropical, hot and humid in summer (28–33°C, 80% RH), modified by the maritime location, dropping to 10°C in the

Castle Peak Power Stations. Architects: RMJM (photo: RMJM).

winter. Special attention was paid to heat loadings from installed plant, and to the provision of temperature- and humidity-controlled environments for sensitive equipment.

The site is located on the shore at the western extremity of the New Territories, vulnerable to typhoons sweeping in from the

South China Sea. Thus particular attention had to be paid to wind-loading, fixing of cladding and glazing against suction, and impact resistance against flying debris. Flat roofs are preferred for easy clearance of gutters when typhoon warnings are given, with oversized gutters designed for gradual discharge of associated heavy rain.

The way of life in Hong Kong is pressurized and entrepreneurial, fast moving, youthful, hard working, but resistant to external ideas. Success is measured in financial terms. Stylistically Hong Kong is aggressively international, with a tradition of local styles only for small domestic buildings. In the design RMJM used details reminiscent of Chinese temples and decorated storage tanks with giant Chinese characters representing their contents (such as water, oil or ash) visible from the nearby aircraft flight path approaching Kai Tak airport.

Sociological aspects affecting the design of the Power Stations included dual catering facilities in Western and Chinese styles, and the design of hazard signs in dual languages, symbols and colours intelligible to local workers.

The *Feng-shui* (or Chinese geomancy) of the site and the adjoining village was very important. Negotiations took place on the form of cut and fill of the rugged terrain to form the site, relocation of graves, moving of crops, etc. to ensure auspicious timing and adequate compensation.

The local building industry had extensive resources of labour, and of materials and products both imported and made locally. High-quality finishes could be achieved, and are well maintained with frequent cleaning and cheap labour.

Fire fighting, means of escape and building regulations are covered in detail under local building ordinances on the basis of UK regulations, adapted to local conditions. British Codes of Practice predominate, but alternatives from the USA, Japan, Europe, etc. are also accepted. APs are expected to be familiar with these, as are local suppliers.

Implementation

Design and production drawings were carried out on the A-Station in the UK by RMJM and Partners through L G Mouchel & Partners (Asia) as APs. For the B-Station production drawings were carried out by RMJM & Partners (Hong Kong) who by this time had individual APs, with the UK partnership as consultants.

During these stages intensive periods of three weeks were set aside every three months for meetings with the client, local authorities and utilities, and presentations to planners and neighbours: and (for the A-Station) with the local Department of Works and local building industry firms to check costings of alternative products and finishes.

Following the negotiation of the GEC plant supply contract, the civil construction was implemented through a series of separate contract packages (e.g. site formation, foundations, superstructure, plant supply and erection). Under the coordination of the CLP project manager, each package was subject to competitive bidding by locally based construction companies. The superstructure packages (with which RMJM were mainly involved) were let to Kumagai Gumi (HK), a Hong Kong contractor with Japanese connections.

The superstructure contracts were supervised by CLP and Mouchel site staff with an expatriate resident architect (from RMJM's UK office) and local support staff. On the B-Station there was an expatriate Clerk of Works in addition.

Changes in drawings and specification were made in the local office, priced and agreed as variations between the client and contractor, and built very rapidly, sometimes being put into effect within 24 hours.

Foremen and supervisors generally spoke English but instructed building operatives in Cantonese, translating specifications and annotations on drawings into Cantonese themselves.

People

Living conditions for expatriates are agreeable if slightly more expensive than the UK (excluding accommodation). Senior staff resident in Hong Kong had married postings, with good local English-speaking schools and social and recreational facilities.

The resident architect lived close to site (about 20 miles from Kowloon) and had the advantage of a Cantonese-speaking wife. Their young children were able to attend a local kindergarten or primary school in Kowloon (both English language), depending on age.

Administration

This was a straightforward job mainly because Hong Kong, as a Crown Colony, operates very much as an extension of the UK. Fees earned in Hong Kong were freely transferable to the UK, and exchange rates over the period did not vary to any great extent. No work permits or visas were needed. The effect of travel for short-term visitors to Hong Kong (through a time-zone change of 8 hours) was not adequately considered: a day's acclimatization should have been allowed. Language was not a problem as all staff in the Hong Kong office and works office, including secretaries and drivers, spoke English.

Main lessons

- The aggressively commercial character of Hong Kong and its particular climate were critical to the project, in selection of staff, in understanding the systems of approvals and the need for APs, and in the selection of materials and products.
- The diligence of building operatives in carrying out the work, and their willingness to remedy defects, helped to achieve rapid and effective results.

Case Study 2: Mbeya Referral Hospital, Tanzania

Design and contract administration of the rehabilitation and redevelopment of existing hospitals as a 460-bed referral and maternity hospital.

Location: South-west Tanzania
Client: Tanzanian Ministry of Health
Value: £8 million (plus equipment £1.25 million)
Funding: ODA
Dates: Appointed 1979

	Start on site	Completion
Staff housing	1979	1980
Maternity hospital	1981	1983
Referral hospital	1982	1989

Team

Norman & Dawbarn (N&D): Project Managers, Architects, Engineers and Medical Facility Planners
Stratton Castell & Partners in association with Armstrong & Duncan (Tanzania): Quantity Surveyors

Business development

N & D had had a branch office in Tanzania since 1960 carrying out projects such as the National University, strategic grain-stores and ODA-funded agricultural housing. They were shortlisted by the Ministry of Works from a long list prepared by the ODA and were selected on the basis of a technical submission (covering approach, CVs of proposed team, and relevant experience). No design or financial submission was required.

Setting up

The Tanzanian-born partner in charge and other senior staff had to be registered to practise locally with the Board of Registration (which accepted RIBA qualifications). The Tanzanian Institute of Architects was formed during the 1980s to represent the interests of architects in practice on similar lines to the RIBA in the UK. There was no requirement for local architect associates or counterparts.

The consultancy contract was signed with ODA and consisted of a simple contractual letter with reference to RIBA and ACE agreements. A lump sum based on man-month rates and estimated time inputs for all disciplines was negotiated. Estimates for all reimbursable expenses were also included. All were based on current costs, and revised annually for inflation and changes in scope of work.

Appropriate design and technology

The local climate is temperate, typical of a tropical plateau at about 1000 m above sea level, with a diurnal temperature range from 0° to 25°C from May to October, and heavy rainfall in January/February making building operations impossible. The site is close to the Rift Valley and thus prone to frequent earthquakes (of magnitude 6–7 on the Richter scale): it is also liable to dust storms in the dry season.

The tradition in Tanzania is for the extended family to

Mbeya Referral Hospital. Architects: Norman & Dawbarn (photo: Norman & Dawbarn).

accompany the patient to hospital and provide food, although in this hospital they are accommodated where necessary in separate hostels run by charities. In the paediatric wing of the main hospital there are training facilities for mothers in cooking and nutrition, in addition to normal wards and delivery suites.

Stylistically the local client wanted a large multi-storey building, similar to others recently completed in Northern Tanzania, with a flat roof, considered as the best European style. However, N&D persuaded them to accept a single-storey pavilion layout due to difficult ground conditions, earthquake hazard, movement of large numbers of people, avoidance of lifts, and to facilitate phasing, with pitched roofs for rapid shedding of rain and to improve internal thermal comfort conditions.

The building industry was labour-intensive, mainly with expatriate-managed European contractors. Apart from cement and aggregates, all materials or components had to be imported and transported by road or rail 700 km from Dar es Salaam. All materials and equipment had either to be local or of British manufacture (to meet ODA funding rules) imported free of duty.

Planning and building regulations were modified British standards administered by the Mbeya Regional Authority. British hospital planning standards were modified to suit the project: e.g. smaller beds and bedspaces to avoid overcrowding which would have resulted from inserting additional beds within British standard bed spaces; the operating theatre had filtered air not full air-conditioning, easier to maintain, and sufficient at that altitude; voltage stabilizers were needed to regulate variations in main electrical supply, and a standby generator to maintain essential supply during periodic interruption; and the British hospital categorization of furniture and equipment supply and installation was modified to suit local conditions. The accent was on robust and simple technology to ensure that the completed hospital could be maintained to the necessary level within the limits of local resources and engineering skills.

Implementation

An initial period was spent in Tanzania by two N&D Partners, drawing up the brief in consultation with ODA expatriate medical advisers, organizing surveys, and preparing the outline design. The full scheme design was then drawn up and costed in the UK, and taken for an extended round of Ministries in Dar es Salaam and the authorities in Mbeya for approval.

The project suffered from being part of a wider ODA-funded integrated rural health project. For example, early in the project the client's Project Manager had been occupied with assembling bicycles for the outreach programme!

The staff housing and the Maternity Hospital were designed in Dar es Salaam with medical planning advice from the UK, being simple in design or consisting of replanning and upgrading existing buildings. The drawings for the Referral Hospital were prepared in the UK for speed and economy in coordinating the more complex design and service requirements. Carefully measured advance orders were placed for long-delivery materials and equipment (e.g. steelwork, steel reinforcing bars, roof sheeting, security fencing, nails). The Development Control Plan ensured that contracts were timed to get building structure and roofs completed in the dry season to facilitate working under shelter during the rainy season, and construction of departments was carefully sequenced to keep the hospital running throughout the building programme.

All contractors were selected by conventional tender methods, although the shortlisting for the Referral Hospital was delayed by extended and detailed consideration by the client. A local contractor was selected for the staff housing, and a UK-registered, Zambian-based, expatriate-managed contractor (Wade Adams Construction Ltd) was selected separately for each of the Maternity and Referral Hospitals.

The contract stage was administered by a resident architect, with support and engineering inspection from Dar es Salaam, and periodic visits by specialists and the partner-in-charge from the UK.

A number of problems arose during contract: delays in clearance of duty-free components through customs; circuitous routing of monthly certificates through several ministries before reaching ODA: intermittent breakdown of telephone and telex and reliance on local buses to carry instructions and messages; and difficulties in getting adequate specialist contractors to the remote site (e.g. for medical gases).

A period of commissioning and training hospital staff was allowed to demonstrate how the new facilities were designed to be run before the hospital was brought into use.

People

The site architect was resident in Mbeya for the duration of the contracts with his family. His children were young enough to be educated at home by his wife. His house also acted as a guest house for visiting senior staff from Dar es Salaam, Nairobi and London. His salary was 40% higher than in the UK, with all local costs found by N&D. There was no tax payable locally (being exempt as the project was funded by ODA). There was a small local expatriate community of 150 or so, and extensive nature and wildlife reserves close at hand for recreation. Local staff consisted of a secretary and driver (both bilingual in English and Swahili), a watchman and a gardener. The site architect needed a work permit which took time to obtain.

Administration

All fees were payable in the UK in £ free of local tax. There were no bonds or advance payment guarantees. Professional indemnity insurance cover was a requirement. ECGD cover was taken out on the project as part of a general N&D policy on all overseas work. The client agreement was drawn up under English law. All documentation was in English, except for official communications from Tanzanian Government offices which were sometimes in Swahili, translated locally.

Main lessons

- It was essential to understand Tanzania's objectives, its administrative procedures, and the psychology and customs of its people.
- It was necessary to provide a Development Control Plan that considered future needs and developments so that future additions relate to the overall functional programme. Some additions have recently been implemented satisfactorily.
- The project was an appropriate design, achieved at a lower cost/bed than the more prestigious referral hospitals of Northern Tanzania, and completed within time and budget, to the total satisfaction of the Ministry of Health and the ODA.
- It was profitable for N&D and professionally satisfying in contributing to a reduced local mortality rate.
- There was considerable benefit in having an established local office in Dar es Salaam, both for local knowledge and as a centre for liaison with the client and other Ministries there.

Case Study 3: Jeddah Corniche, Saudi Arabia

Planning and design of 95 km of dual three-lane road along the shores of the Red Sea extending the waterfront of Jeddah to the north and south.

Location: Kingdom of Saudi Arabia
Client: Municipality of Jeddah and Ministry of Municipal
                 and Rural Affairs
Value: £375 million
Funding: Kingdom of Saudi Arabia
Dates: Appointed 1976
                 Design completed 1977
                 Project completed 1981

Team

RMJM: Architects, Planners, Civil Engineers, Landscape Architects, Quantity Surveyors
Jamieson Mackay & Partners: Transportation and Highway Engineers
University of Wales: Marine Ecology Consultants
   together with local Planners and Engineers seconded from the Ministry

Business development

RMJM had prepared a Master Plan for Jeddah (following the Regional Plan for the Western Region of Saudi Arabia) which identified the coastline of the Red Sea as a unique attraction for the environmental and recreational needs of the city, for which plans needed to be drawn up. RMJM & Partners' Jeddah branch office was appointed to carry out surveys and prepare designs.

Setting up

At appointment the professional disciplines of architect and planner were not recognized in Saudi Arabia, and were included under the description of engineer: nor was professional service recognized as distinct from the provision of goods. There are still no Saudi professional qualifications in these disciplines.

During mobilization the government required all professionals on government assignments to submit CVs and certificates of academic and professional qualifications translated into Arabic and authenticated by the British Embassy and Client Ministry. European and American qualifications were acceptable.

Negotiations of the client agreement and setting up were eased by RMJM already having a planning office in Jeddah. Work permits needed for expatriates were slow in coming through and depended on presenting a signed contract. No local partner or agent was needed on this project, but these had to be introduced on later projects: see Case Study 12.

Appropriate design and technology

The climate is described in Case Study 7. The principal sociological factor was the ownership of the land bordering the sea, and of the foreshore. The study area was about ½km wide, with a large number of villas in private ownership, each owning a strip of beach. Geotechnical surveys revealed a shallow shelf reaching out to coral reefs up to ½km offshore, which was in government ownership. The choice of running the road behind the villas or on reclaimed land on their seaward side was a matter of

Jeddah Corniche. Architects: RMJM (photo: RMJM).

the relative prestige of the owners and appropriate compensation.

Possibilities of recreational use were limited by Muslim social conventions, particularly those affecting women.

North American standards for lane widths, roundabouts, parking, etc. were adopted to suit the predominantly large size of cars owned locally.

Implementation

The expatriate team of ten was set up for the 18-month study period under a RMJM associate project director in the Jeddah office, with local staff, four or five seconded Saudi staff and specialist consultants in marine biology, geotechnics and arid zone planting.

In due course the road was designed in detail by Sautechnic (an Italian civil engineering consultant) from RMJM's 1/1000 plans and detailed sections, and constructed (but not under RMJM supervision). The designs were deliberately made for slow speeds with frequent roundabouts and relatively tight bends. Separated carriageways allowed the landside road section to be raised above the seaside road, thus allowing better seaviews. Sites were designated for shaded car parks and occasional lagoons, and for future recreational buildings (including a bathysphere for Muslim women to observe the submarine environment of the coral reefs!).

People

Senior staff were resident with their families, and junior staff and technicians on bachelor postings, dictated partly by work permits and partly by the tightness of the fee. Women were not allowed to work, except in limited medical and educational occupations, or in the Embassy or British Council offices. Nor were they allowed to drive, so drivers were needed to go shopping or take children to school.

Expatriate staff were paid 30% more than the UK, but had no local taxation apart from 5% contribution to GOSI (The Government Social Security Tax). Leave periods were eight calendar weeks per year (including one each during the Hadj and Ramadan). Staff on bachelor assignments lived in shared flats with individual bedrooms and communal living rooms, and these flats also accommodated visiting partners from the UK office. Although seconded staff were all Saudi graduates from different foreign universities, some very able, it was time consuming training them and involving them productively in the team.

All reports, correspondence and accounts had to be in Arabic as well as English, an essential contribution by a technical translator and by bilingual local staff (from Palestine, Egypt and Jordan).

Administration

The fee was negotiated as a fixed lump sum including expenses, expatriate and local staff, seconded staff, office, transport, housing, air fares and children's schooling for expatriates. Thus a careful analysis was needed of the risks and contingencies which might arise, and of local costs. Expenses accounted for nearly 50% of the total lump sum fee.

Payment of fees and expenses was staged in relation to the design of each section of road, and dependent on Ministry approval of proposals. Advance payment was made against a guarantee (which was taken by the bank as a liability against the facility offered) and repaid by reducing each fee claim by an equivalent proportion. A Performance Bond (5% of the total fee) had to be given, and maintained throughout the project, as a Bank Guarantee which could be called by the client on demand. The Bond could only be released by the following in sequence:

(1) Written approval of all the work by the Ministry.
(2) Completion and audit of RMJM accounts for the year in which final fee payment was to be made (not the year due!).
(3) Payment of tax and issue of up-to-date tax certificate.
(4) Payment of final fee.
(5) Release of Performance Bond.

Bureaucratic delays led to tax certificates being out of date by the time they were issued, which was only remedied by hiring a local tax attorney (with influence in the local tax office) to obtain timely certificates so that the Performance Bond could be released.

A decision had to be made early in the project as to whether to opt for corporation tax on turnover or profit. A Double Taxation Agreement exists between Saudi Arabia and the UK.

There was no exchange control on fees earned in the country, and the exchange rate changed in RMJM's favour from over 8 to under 6 Saudi Riyals to the pound, which assisted in the project's profitability. ECGD cover was taken out against risks of non-payment and non-remittance.

A long 57-hour week was worked (0800–18.30 with two-hour lunch break, 5.5 days/week with a Muslim weekend) often with client presentations in the evening in addition. Thus few expatriates had time to learn more than a few words of Arabic.

Main lessons

- A careful risk assessment and analysis of likely costs had to be done before negotiating and agreeing the fixed lump-sum fee.
- Accounts and tax filing had to be up to date to obtain release of the performance bond.

- Staff had to be carefully chosen to live and work happily within the family and social constraints of the country.
- Good bilingual local staff were essential to the timely presentation of reports and accounts, and the day-to-day running of the office.
- Although written reports were necessary (having been specified in the Agreement) in practice the client was mainly concerned with drawings, and took the reports as read.

Case Study 4: Kota Kinabalu Air Terminal, East Malaysia

Design and contract administration of a new terminal building for the existing airport.

Location: Sabah, East Malaysia.
Client: The Government of Malaysia
Value: MR 53 million (approx. £23 million on completion).
Dates: Appointed for Master Plan 1968
              Brief Preparation 1973
              Start on site 1980
              Completion 1985

Team

RMJM & Partners: Architect sub-consultants to
    Scott Wilson Kirkpatrick & Partners (SWKP): Civil Engineers
Architects Team 3 (AT3) later Jurubena Bertiga: Associate
    Architects
Preece Cardew and Rider: Building Services Engineers
Franklin & Andrews (in association with Pakatan International):
    Quantity Surveyors

Business development

RMJM were approached by SWKP following joint working on schools in Singapore and transportion projects in Hong Kong.

Setting up

The architectural profession in Malaysia is well developed on the lines of the profession in the UK. The local professional body Pertubuhan Akitek Malaysia (PAM) publishes Codes of Conduct, Forms of Agreement, Scales of Professional Conduct, etc. and is a member of the Commonwealth Association of Architects. RMJM formed an association for executive work for relevant stages of work on the project with AT3.

Appropriate design and technology

The site is at sea-level (+2.7 m), tropical, very hot and humid, with heavy monsoon rains. It is in an occasional earthquake zone, on a site filled over former mangrove swamps.

The principal social influences derive from the remoteness of the site from the Federal capital in Kuala Lumpur (1000 miles west across the South China Sea), while forming an important node of communication with adjoining countries (Hong Kong, the Philippines, Brunei and Indonesia) and remote local airports in Sabah. Aircraft to be handled varied from wide-bodied jets to small turbo-props. Initial projections of air movements were higher than for Kuala Lumpur: this caused funding difficulties between Federal and State authorities in the programming of investment in airport projects. Initially designed to be naturally ventilated (high ceilings, narrow cross-section) it was eventually air-conditioned. Stylistically the client preference was for an international design.

There was a limited local building industry, with most material and components imported through the nearby port, difficulties with local aggregates, plentiful local unskilled labour, good local welders (ex-oil industry), and other tradesmen imported. Federal Codes of Practice (mainly UK-based) were not always adjusted to local conditions.

Project implementation

The initial design was mainly done in the UK (to suit consultancy location). Production and tender information was prepared by local associates in Kuala Lumpur (except civil and structural engineering done in the UK which caused problems of coordination and delays). No local Sabahan contractor had adequate capability so national and South-east Asian firms were prequalified, and a Chinese-led firm from West Malaysia was eventually appointed, on a PAM version of the JCT 63 contract.

There was a conflict between international quality (needed for prestige and operational reasons) and local achievement possible and affordable. This particularly applied to electrical/mechanical and communications sub-contracts.

Kota Kinabalu Air Terminal. Architects: RMJM (photo: RMJM).

People

The only RMJM resident expatriate staff were the architect who prepared the brief over a period of several months (during which he met his future wife!) and two successive resident site architects during construction. With no local staff each was responsible for paying personal local tax, keeping financial records, bank account, etc. There was a small salary mark-up (of 10%) over UK levels, paid locally in Malaysian Ringgit, with considerable benefit to individuals as the MR strengthened against the £ sterling. Living conditions for expatriates were good with a reasonably sized expatriate community, golf and yacht clubs, hash harriers (hare and hounds) etc. Work permits and visas were needed from state authorities.

Administration

The fee agreement was favourable with setting-up payments without bond guarantee. Withholding tax was introduced later deducting 15% tax from each fee payment. This was only released with evidence on production of personal tax certificates for expatriate staff and RMJM's profit and loss accounts verified by local accountants. Fees were paid locally in MR, without restriction on remittance to UK.

Main lessons

- This was a rewarding and satisfactory job, albeit over a much longer period (over 11 years from briefing to handover) than expected at the outset.
- We had the great advantage of a sympathetic client trained within the British education system, sharing our sense of humour, etc.
- It is important to understand the Malay culture, and the meaning of words.
- Difficulties arose over ambiguities of client authority and objectives (between Federal and State).
- We suffered the adverse effect on the project of the UK

Government's decision to increase fees for Malaysian (and other foreign) students at British institutions of higher and further education (plus routeing disagreements between the governments over traffic rights for British Airways and Malaysian Airline Systems between Kuala Lumpur and London Heathrow) leading to a "look East/buy British last" policy by the Malaysian government.

- There were difficulties for SWKP as project leaders due to the greater status of the architect in Malay eyes with the client seeing this as a building project rather than pure civil engineering.

Case Study 5:
The Jamahiriya Museum, Tripoli, Libya

Design and contract administration of a new museum of history and archaeology within the historic Assaray Al-Hamra citadel (the Red Castle).

Location: Libya
Client: Department of Antiquities
Value: $30 million
Funding: Libyan Government
Dates: Appointed 1981
              Museum opened 1988

Team

RMJM: Architects, Engineers, Quantity Surveyors and Project
  Managers
Higgins, Ney & Partners: Interior Design/Museum Consultants

Business development

RMJM had been working in Libya since the early 1970s on a new township near Tripoli for 5000 dwellings and related physical and social infrastructure, central area planning, urban roads, abattoir complex and cold stores in Misurata, and roads in Western Libya, among other work which carried on into the mid-1980s.

In 1981 RMJM were appointed (after shortlist and interview) to review a design prepared by American consultants under the auspices of UNESCO and to act as project managers for alterations to this museum. Site investigations by the contractors revealed inadequacies in the existing structure, leading to its demolition and to a design for a new enlarged museum being prepared by RMJM in 1982.

Setting up

At the outset there were no local consultancy practices, nor any distinction between consultants and contractors, nor between engineers and architects. Individual British architects and engineers had to register with the local Engineering Society for which notarized professional certificates from the UK were required.

RMJM & Partners established a branch office in Tripoli registered for local work in Libya, and carried out the project as lead executive consultants for all skills, with Higgins Ney as

The Jamahiriya Museum. Architects: RMJM (photo: RMJM).

interior/exhibition sub-consultants (who had a direct appointment to UNESCO, but were not registered to work in Libya). As
already indicated, there were no local consultants. The Agreement with the client was based on a standard UNESCO format.

Appropriate design and technology

The local climate is sub-tropical Mediterranean with marine
humidity and air-borne salt. The area is mildly seismic, with
high sulphate levels in the ground. Stylistically the design is
traditional to fit in with the historic Red Castle.

The indigenous building industry is traditionally based and
labour-intensive, using local limestone and concrete blocks, and
rendering. All other materials, components and equipment are
imported. Maintenance is a local problem, particularly of
building services and equipment. Standards and codes are
based on American and British practice.

Implementation

Design, production and tender information stages were carried
out in the UK and an excellent Scandinavian contractor was
appointed from a European shortlist by conventional tender,
with good skilled tradesmen (from Pakistan, Thailand and the
Philippines). Site administration was carried out by an all-
British team representing all professional disciplines with a
Clerk of Works.

People

In the 1970s senior staff were resident with families. However,
for this project most staff were on long- or short-term bachelor
contracts, due partly to lack of adequate expatriate schooling
above primary level and partly to the poor quality of life (the
result of shortages of commodities and limited varieties of food
and consumer goods).

Personal contracts were for 10 weeks in Libya with 2 weeks'
holiday. During construction rather basic accommodation was

provided within the contractor's compound, with club and recreation facilities. Working hours were long (12 hours/day).

Individuals were paid about 80% more than in the UK to compensate for severance from families and hardship. All salaries and benefits-in-kind (including a proportion of housing) were liable to Libyan income tax, and had to be declared monthly to enable employees to remit 90% of net salary.

It was essential to have a senior representative, with delegated authority and lots of stamina and some facility in speaking Arabic. Local bilingual staff were important, especially to translate all letters and reports into Arabic, and to obtain immigration visas and work permits.

Administration

Under the agreement fees and UK expenses were paid by UNESCO in $. In the event the successful financial out-turn of the project was due in some part to favourable fluctuation of exchange rates. All local payments had to be made through the nationalized bank which led to laborious bureaucratic delays. No overdrafts were permitted, and no interest was payable on balances, so remittance delays were costly.

The firm was liable to corporate tax on profits declared annually for the firm's business in Libya as a whole. Several years later the tax authorities audited the firm's books (which had to be kept in Arabic) and raised a final tax, which was punitive, for example on disallowing overseas expenditure, with low chances of success on appeal.

ECGD cover was available (and cheaper than private alternatives) up to 1982, and provided most useful cover against delays in remittance. The lack of availability of cover subsequently raises questions about the viability of any future work.

All local activities were liable to the local Libyan legal system with no private lawyers allowed to act for individuals or for the firm.

Main lessons

- UNESCO's technical and administrative involvement was crucial.

- The building was well built by an excellent contractor with skilled expatriate tradesmen.
- The project depended on competent and committed staff on the ground.
- Appropriate personalities of senior staff and lack of interference from the UK head office were crucial to the success of the project.

Case Study 6: UNESCAP Conference Centre, Bangkok, Thailand

Design and contract administration of a new Conference Centre for the United Nations at the headquarters of the Economic and Social Commission for Asia and the Pacific.

Location: Bangkok, Thailand
Client: United Nations
Value: $37.5 million
Funding: United Nations
Dates: Competition 1984
              Under construction 1992

Team

M L Tri Devakul/RMJM and Associates (MLTD/RMJM): Architects and Interior Designers
RKV Engineering Consultants: Structural Engineers
Prasat & Visvakorn/RMJM: Environmental Engineers
Sandy Brown Associates: Acoustics Consultants
SGS/ Construction Cost Consultants (Bangkok): Quantity Surveyors (post-competition)

Business development

RMJM had been working in Thailand in the early 1970s designing and supervising the Chancery building for the British

Embassy, and the Master Plan and first phase of the Asian Institute of Technology. In the early 1980s as part of a business development exercise in South-east Asia RMJM considered that Thailand offered promising opportunities as a country with good political stability and economic prospects.

In 1983 RMJM set up a joint venture company with M L Tri Devakul in Bangkok, which early in 1984 responded to a local advertisement for an international competition for the new building. MLTD/RMJM put in a submission of interest and were one of four teams short-listed, out of 80 international teams which submitted. The competition entry was prepared in Bangkok as a joint Anglo-Thai effort, with senior design architects and engineers from the UK and an enthusiastic team of local architects, modelmakers and perspective artists working a 70-hour week to meet the high standards of presentation needed to win.

MLTD/RMJM were finally selected late in 1984. One of the conditions of the competition was to carry out the project for a fee of 5% of construction cost (up to tender) for architects and engineers.

UNESCAP Conference Centre. Architects: M L Tri Devakul / RMJM (photo: MLTD/RMJM).

Setting up

The architectural profession is recognized in Thailand and regulated by the Siam Institute of Architects, on lines similar to the RIBA and ARCUK in the UK. All consultations on planning and building regulation matters were carried out by the Thai member of MLTD/RMJM.

An inter-firm Agreement was signed for the project agreeing the sharing of tasks and responsibilities at each stage, and how payments of fees and expenses would be shared. Local (mainly expatriate) quantity surveyors were appointed by the client direct, first to cost the shortlisted competition submissions, and then to carry out normal services on the project.

An Agreement with the United Nations was negotiated and signed in mid-1985 in New York and Bangkok (on a UN form of contract), defining in detail the services to be provided, with a schedule of staged payments.

Appropriate design and technology

Thailand has a hot-humid tropical climate with heavy monsoon rains. The site is located in the centre of Bangkok on an alluvial plain which is subsiding at a significant rate (estimated at 1.5 m over the last 30 years), so that the flooding associated with annual rains and high tides in the Gulf of Thailand is becoming progressively more acute. This necessitates a deep-piled structure, with discontinuity at the perimeter, and entry to basement parking over raised bunds.

The client welcomed the attempt to reflect in the design the predominant Thai and regional characteristics of overlapping roof forms, while respecting the mainly low- to medium-height buildings of the nearby historic buildings. The local building industry was experienced in medium-sized projects with high levels of craftsmanship in timber, concrete and roof tiling. Most specialist components and equipment and materials such as marble were imported.

The project has diplomatic status and was therefore exempt from conforming to local Thai regulations for planning permission and building regulation control. Local regulations for fire fighting and means of escape were inadequate for the international standards required by the UN: the choice lay between American or British standards so with the client's agreement RMJM, being more familiar with the former Greater London Council regulations for places of assembly, designed in accordance with these and submitted the scheme to an independent fire consultant for certification.

Implementation

There was some duality between the two parts of the client body: the headquarters in New York and the immediate user in Bangkok. In practice, the strategic decisions (overall scope, budget, brief, programme) were made in New York, and detailed approvals of design and tenders took place in Bangkok. Frequent audio tele-conferences were set up between Bangkok and New York to expedite design decisions.

All design and production work was carried out in Bangkok, as the majority of the design team and the immediate user client were based there. The team consisted of a senior RMJM project director, architects and engineers and a powerhouse of Thai architects, interior designers and engineers, with British acoustic consultants making short visits.

A delay of over two years ensued before tenders were called, owing to funding problems for UN capital projects. Selection of the contractor followed normal practice of prequalifying major local contractors and international/Thai consortia (to maximize expatriate management knowhow with local labour and craft expertise), followed by tender by shortlisted contractors and consortia based on Bills of Quantities and drawings. In the event, the contractor selected was a local Thai firm. The contract has run into delays due to the overheating of the local building industry.

Supervision on site is provided by a USA-trained Thai engineer and an expatriate architect, with Thai inspectors provided by MLTD/RMJM and other members of the design team, under the direction of RMJM's office in Hong Kong.

People

Selection of the project manager and senior architects to be resident in Bangkok with wives and families was critically important. Bangkok is a lively and sophisticated metropolis with good English-language schools and a large international community.

Thai is a difficult language to learn to speak or read, so local bilingual staff were essential both within and outside the office. Local drivers were needed to help cope with the appalling traffic in Bangkok.

Salaries paid to resident expatriate staff were about 30% above UK levels, and were liable to local taxation.

Administration

It was only possible to carry out the project profitably for such a low fee because of the high productivity of the team, and the lower salary levels of local architects and draughtsmen in comparison with expatriates. The Agreement was negotiated in such a way that income from fees and expenses in Bangkok and overseas respectively (paid in Baht in Bangkok and $ in Singapore) balanced expenditure as near as possible. Unfortunately the strengthening of the £ against the $ (by up to 30%) and against the Baht (which is closely related to the $) over the period of the project has adversely affected its profitability.

ECGD cover was not taken out on the project because of the prestigious client and lack of restrictions on exchange control. The joint venture was liable to pax tax (on declared profit), but there is a Double Taxation Agreement between the UK and Thailand.

An expatriate British lawyer and partner of one of the leading legal practices in Bangkok was retained at the outset to advise on the selection of a Local Associate and on the joint venture agreement (drafted under Thai laws). The Client Agreement was drafted under US law, and the building contract followed UN forms, without stating a law of jurisdiction.

Main lessons

- By setting up a joint venture company in Thailand we were well placed to learn of, and respond to, the international competition for this project.
- The partnership of RMJM's approach to design for a public client and the Thai associate's local design sensitivity was a crucial factor in winning the competition.
- It took more time than anticipated to combine the international experience of the senior expatriate staff with the local experience and skills of the Thai staff.
- The extended delay before tender (when the production team had to be disbanded) led to problems as the contract administration team had to be built up from scratch without background knowledge of the project, or of the working method of the local consultants.
- The largest factor which affected the project's profitability was the hardening of the £ against the $ and the Baht over the extended period.

Case Study 7: Al Balad Historic Area, Jeddah, Saudi Arabia

A detailed study of the 150 ha historic core of the City of Jeddah as part of an advisory role under an overall technical assistance programme.

Location: Kingdom of Saudi Arabia
Client: Municipality of Jeddah
Dates: Appointed 1980
             Completed 1988

Team

RMJM (Saudi Arabia): Architects and Planners
Jamieson Mackay & Partners: Transportation Engineers
    in association with a seconded Saudi team of architects, engineers and technicians

Business development

RMJM were selected in 1970, following shortlisting and interview by a committee set up by the United Nations at the request of the Saudi Ministry of the Interior, to prepare a Physical Plan for the Western Region and Master Plans for five major cities in it (including Jeddah, Mecca and Medina). The conservation project was one of several assignments which followed from the Master Plan for Jeddah.

Setting up

The project was carried out by RMJM (Saudi Arabia) a partnership based in the Channel Islands and registered in Saudi Arabia. Partners included some of the British partners and some senior staff resident in Saudi Arabia, including an Arabic-speaking Jordanian. Architects, engineers and planners had no status in the country at the start of the project, and indeed no professional institutions exist there today, except in the form of learned societies. The concept of professional service was not understood at the outset, and Agreements were the same as for goods, prepared in Arabic and interpreted under Sharia (*Koranic*) law. Scale fees were thus unknown, and had to be expressed either as lump-sum or man-month rates, or a combination of these. Since these could not be exceeded, a very clear statement of services was needed, with a detailed analysis of potential risks to be anticipated.

Appropriate design and technology

Jeddah has a tropical desert climate, with long hot humid summers, low rainfall, cooling sea breezes one day in three, and dust storms 30 days in the year. Response to this climate and to the Muslim way of life and the mercantile traditions gave the centre of the city a character and vitality which the client wished to conserve as the historic port of entry to the Kingdom, particularly for pilgrims undertaking the *Hadj*. This was a key element in the expansion over 40 years of a walled town of some 30 000 people to a metropolitan city of 1.7 million people.

The assignment included an exhaustive study and grading of the existing building and local craft skills, and the development of new uses for buildings, constructional standards, and building regulations.

Al Balad Historic Area: Architects RMJM (photo: John French).

Implementation

The project was carried out by a team resident in Jeddah from start to finish. The team's role initially was to survey and record, to plan how buildings could be conserved; then to carry out demonstration projects, supervise the upgrading of public utilities, roads, street furniture, paths and open spaces (in the ownership of the Municipality); and approve the conservation of individual buildings.

People

Initially all staff were accompanied by wives and children: however, gradually this only applied to senior staff, with junior staff on bachelor status. Wives could only obtain appropriate jobs in the health and education sector and were not allowed to drive or engage in sports in public. Despite these restrictions, the posting was popular with staff. The project director's wife and the principal client's wife became such friends that they exchanged English/Arabic lessons to their mutual benefit and understanding!

There was no local personal taxation, except social security tax of 13% part paid by RMJM and part by individuals.

Salaries had a mark-up (40%) over UK levels and were paid locally in Saudi Riyals, with benefit to individuals as the SR strengthened against the £.

Administration

The project director was responsible for financial control and profitability, including technical and administrative costs. On earlier jobs we had been subject to 10% performance bonds (as applicable to contracts for goods) which had proved extremely difficult to get released. After years of combined efforts by British (and other national) consultants, the Saudi government eventually dispensed with performance bonds for all consulting contracts. Thus no bonds were needed on this project.

Timely preparation and certified audited accounts were essential to obtain final fee payments, showing that company tax had been paid. Fees were paid in SR, and freely convertible to £.

The legal system is based on the Sharia (*Koranic*) code; under this code, for example, an owner cannot be prevented from giving "life" to his land, even though this takes the form of what we would term "development". Also generous compensation is due to an owner whose land is required for, say, a new road.

All communications and reports had to be in Arabic, and in practice were prepared and submitted in Arabic and English.

Main lessons

- It is vital to select the right people to live overseas. They must have technical ability, personal commitment and have an appropriate personality (although this is inevitably subjective).
- Full commitment to working overseas is essential at partner/ director level both at home and overseas.
- Full authority and financial accountability must be excercised by the project director.
- No two countries (even in the Arab world) are the same. It is essential that a company starting to work or quoting for work fully understands the legal and contractual requirements as well as how to fulfil the technical brief for the country in question.

Case Study 8: Century Tower, Tokyo, Japan

Design and contract administration of a new office building in the centre of Tokyo.

Location: Japan
Client: Century Real Estate
Size: 25 000 m²
Funding: Private
Dates: Appointed 1986
              Completed 1991

Team

Foster Associates (now Sir Norman Foster & Partners): Architects
Ove Arup & Partners (OAP): Structural ⎫
  Engineers   ⎬ to completion of
J Roger Preston & Partners: Building ⎰ scheme design
  Services Engineers
Northcroft and Nicholson: Quantity Surveyors

Business development

Fosters had visited Japan in connection with the Headquarters Building for the Hongkong and Shanghai Bank (HKSB) in Hong Kong, and were keen to work in Japan. They were approached by the client, on the basis of their established international reputation.

Setting up

The architectural profession is recognized in Japan and regulated by the Japan Institute of Architects. However, the majority of architects are employed by contractors and design-and-build predominates as the preferred method of procuring buildings. It is also common for independent architects to design buildings, after which a contractor with his professional staff obtain approvals, prepare production information and carry through construction. On this project the client had already appointed Ohbayashi (one of the "big six" contractors) to work on the project, as they had been associated with earlier buildings on the site for over 50 years. However, Fosters wished to be fully involved in every stage of the project from briefing to completion, including working closely with the constructors of the building and its components, which is central to their design philosophy.

Foster Associates were appointed as executive architects, and opened a liaison office in Tokyo upon appointment. The other consultants had direct appointments, Fosters acting as paymasters.

Appropriate design and technology

Tokyo has a temperate and humid climate but is subject to typhoons and torrential rains in September. It is also liable to earthquakes, and has rigorous seismic codes to which all new buildings have to be designed. Stylistically the Japanese are conservative, but the client wanted an expressive building with the Foster hallmark. A feature was made of an innovative eccentrically braced column structure proposed by OAP, to survive earthquakes.

The building industry is dominated by six large contractors, who in turn coordinate a large but fragmented series of sub-contractors. They are committed to producing and taking responsibility for the highest quality of finished product, which thereby reduces the architect's professional liability. When

Century Tower. Architects: Sir Norman Foster & Partners (photo: Ian Lambot).

Fosters started work construction costs were broadly similar to London, since when costs in Japan have risen faster than in the UK.

Building regulations are complicated and more variable than in the UK, covering, for example, a narrow comfort range (in temperature and relative humidity) for the interior, which has to be monitored and reported on in use. Japanese architects normally conform to regulations rather than argue against them: thus Fosters and OAP together with Ohbayashi's architects and engineers had to negotiate slowly and patiently to achieve agreement to depart from regulations where needed by the innovative design (for example, the structure, the narrow atrium, and free-standing glass lifts). The project was specified and built to JIS standards, with which Fosters were already familiar from the HKSB Headquarters in Hong Kong.

Implementation

The development of the design into production information was carried out in the UK, with frequent communication by telephone and facsimile with the liaison office (and thus the client and Ohbayashi) in Tokyo. The centre of gravity of the project then moved to Tokyo, with the UK office in an advisory role. Advantage was taken of the time-change between London and Tokyo of 9 hours to achieve effectively a 21-hour working day. Drawings and floppy disks were passed to and fro by courier.

Bearing in mind Fosters' philosophy of close working in the development of the design with the sub-contractors, and the role of Ohbayashi's architects and engineers in getting approvals, preparing detailed engineering drawings and coordinating sub-contractors' design and fabrication drawings, this was a complex operation. It relied on the similar method which had already been perfected for building the HKSB Headquarters in Hong Kong and other Fosters' projects. All drawings had to be completed and building control approval obtained before work started on site. All annotations and specifications were issued from the UK in English, and translated where necessary into Japanese in Tokyo.

Once work had started, on-site inspection was carried out

from the liaison office in Tokyo, with occasional visits from the UK, at a level similar to the RIBA's normal service. It was not found necessary to employ a Clerk of Works as the contractor's supervision and quality control was of the highest, often condemning workmanship which Fosters might have accepted, or proposing alternatives at no extra cost. Fosters have a separate contract for the fit-out of the offices.

People

Fosters have set up their local office in Tokyo with a director and three senior architects with their families, with houses or apartments, at salaries about twice the UK level. There is no restriction on wives working although opportunities are less than at home because of the position of women in society.

Tokyo is the second most expensive city in the world to live in (after Tehran), about a third more than London (excluding housing).

Expatriates are liable for tax on income arising in Japan. One member of staff learnt Japanese, although translating proved easier than understanding! Bilingual secretaries in London and Tokyo carried out most of the translation of documents into Japanese.

Administration

The fee scale agreed for the project was on a percentage fee basis following the normal RIBA scale, as most of the work was being carried out in the UK, with normal expenses paid as in the UK. Thus the additional costs of staff living in Tokyo were digested within the fee. Japanese national corporation tax, local inhabitants tax and local business tax were levied on the firm's local office. Fees paid were freely convertible into sterling. No ECGD cover was taken out on the project. Contracts were drawn up under Japanese law, but litigation is unusual in Japan. Administration was straightforward, and local accountants were retained to do tax filing and obtain working visas.

Main lessons

- The project suited Fosters' design and working methods very well, with an innovative building of high quality as the outcome.
- Many of the lessons learnt on the HKSB Headquarters in Hong Kong enabled this project to proceed more smoothly.
- It is essential to recognize and respect the particular characteristics of the Japanese: honesty, personal pride, patience, respect and hard work: conservative but progressive.
- Quality is taken for granted in Japan by contractor and craftsmen alike. Thus there is no need for elaborate QA procedures.

Case Study 9: CIMA Branch Office, Colombo, Sri Lanka

Consultancy advice on the procurement of a branch office and study centre for the Chartered Institute of Management Accountants.

Location: Sri Lanka
Client: Chartered Institute of Management Accountants (CIMA)
Value: £200 000
Funding: CIMA (UK)
Dates: Appointed 1986
             Building completed 1988

Team

RMJM: Consultant Architects and Building Services Engineers
Design Consortium Ltd (DCL): Architects, Engineers and
  Quantity Surveyors

Business development

RMJM were approached by CIMA to provide technical advice on this project at the suggestion of DCL (who had been associated with RMJM on an Asian Development Bank Technical Education preparation mission to Sri Lanka in 1981). Since the project was being funded from the UK, CIMA (UK) wished to retain consultants to oversee the project on its behalf.

Setting up

RMJM's role on this project was consultative and non-executive. Architects are fully recognized and regulated by the Sri Lanka Institute of Architects in a similar manner to RIBA and ARCUK in the UK.

One of RMJM's first tasks was to formalize the appointment of DCL as executive consultants to CIMA (Sri Lanka) following a feasibility study prepared by them. RMJM's appointment was on a time-basis against a ceiling of fees and expenses, kept under periodic review.

Appropriate design and technology

Sri Lanka has a hot-humid tropical climate with high monsoon rains, and the site in Colombo is about two miles from the sea, benefiting to some extent from diurnal sea breezes.

The project arose because of great demand by students of accountancy for a professional qualification – a highly marketable and exportable commodity in Sri Lanka's economic circumstances. This put pressure on CIMA's local library (books sometimes being referred to in shifts 24 hours a day), study space, lecture and examination rooms and rooms for qualified members of the Institute. During this period the country was suffering from terrorism by Tamil separatists, directed at random at targets in Colombo.

Stylistically local architects wish to break away from the former colonial style, but retain large well-shaded openings and rapid disposal of monsoon rains in their designs. The local building industry was well equipped to deal with this medium-sized reinforced concrete frame construction, with most materials and craft skills readily available, and a plentiful supply of labour. However, the labourers came from remote villages and lived on site during construction, frequently departing home when terrorist danger threatened.

Planning procedures and building regulations were based on

CIMA Branch Office. Architects: Design Consortium Ltd (photo: CIMA).

UK precedents, although with some flexibility in interpretation. British Standards were specified but the general level of application (e.g. on asbestos and energy conservation) was analogous to that in the UK some 25 years earlier.

Implementation

The key question was how to economize on RMJM's time and expensive visits to Sri Lanka. This was resolved by making two visits each of about a week's duration. The first at the outset was to get local consultants appointed, refine the brief, agree a preliminary design and budget, and set up procedures for reporting up to and after contract. The second, about three-quarters of the way through contract, was to inspect quality, advise on schemes for furniture and decoration, contractual claims and arrangements for handover and official opening by the President of Sri Lanka. During the project several delays took place due to a stop-order by the planning authority for a technical infringement, shortage of steel, and civil unrest.

Work in the UK was carried out on reports and documents sent by courier via CIMA (Sri Lanka): advice was given on the final design, production information, report on tenders, appointment of contractor and periodic reports on progress and certification.

The viability of the project from CIMA (UK)'s point of view was enhanced by the hardening of the £ against the Rupee over the project from 38 to 60 Rupees/£ at a rate much higher than local inflation.

People

The use on this project of senior staff, with wide experience of the whole process of procuring a building in the UK, and similarly overseas, was essential to providing an effective and economic service to the client.

Administration

In effect, this project was little different from one in the UK, and all fees and expenses were paid in the UK in sterling. It was zero-rated for VAT as it was concerned with an overseas building.

It was crucial to have rapid and effective communication with Sri Lanka, which relied initially on telex and courier. The availability of facsimile in DCL's office in mid-1987 greatly speeded up the process. The main difficulties arose through the local CIMA office's reluctance at time to send regular or up-to-date reports.

Main lessons

- This is an example of a small but effective way of exporting architectural expertise, and providing technical advice at arm's length.
- RMJM's involvement ensured that the brief fully represented the client's needs, and that the eventual building provided for them.

- The hardening of the £ against the Rupee enabled a large number of delays and claims to be digested within the original sterling budget.
- It is important to use consultancy techniques which are appropriate and acceptable locally.

Case Study 10: Vargem Fresca, Portugal

Master plan and infrastructure design for a 540 ha site to contain two golf courses, a 5-star 250-bed hotel, sporting and marine leisure areas and an agro-forestry science park.

Location: Near Lisbon, Portugal
Client: Portucale
Value: £120 million
Funding: Private
Dates: Appointed 1991

Team

RMJM (London): Planners, Landscape Architects
EGF-SAGE: Associate Planners, Economists, Civil Engineers

Business development

We researched the most promising European country for our first European base and settled on Portugal. We then went on an Anglo-Portuguese Chamber of Commerce mission, followed six months later by a BCB mission. This gave us a number of contacts and leads which were serious enough to proceed with further visits to interview potential Local Associates and investigate the business environment in more depth, which led to an opportunity to bid for this project.

An initial appraisal was made of the budget to aim at, and inputs and outputs tailored accordingly. Local professional costs are about two-thirds those in the UK. The client is owned one-third by an investment bank, one-third by the local landowner and one-third by British interest groups including agricultural ones.

Setting up

The professions of architecture and planning are still relatively in their infancy with many small architectural firms but few planners. The Local Associates selected wish to expand in size and experience. A simple protocol of inter-firm Agreement covers the project, responsibilities, project direction, and fee payments.

Appropriate design and technology

There are few approved plans for rural areas. Proposals are reviewed by the local municipality and then passed for approval to regional and national authorities. The main standards applicable are EC standards for water and sewage, and those affecting various aspects of agriculture. Mapping was prepared compatible with AUTOCAD.

Implementation

Initial design work was carried out in the UK, where the RMJM team was based, with short visits to Portugal for local liaison, leading to outline planning approval. The work will move so as to be based mainly in Portugal for the design of infrastructure and the obtaining of detailed approvals, done chiefly by the Local Associates. In the event, more assistance to the Local Associates proved necessary than was anticipated by RMJM, owing to local pressure of work and lack of experience.

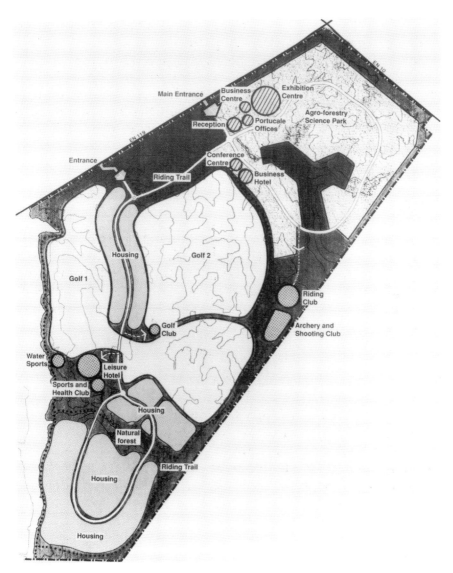

Vargem Fresca. Architects: RMJM (drawing: RMJM).

People

Only senior and experienced RMJM team members travelled to Portugal to maintain liaison with the client and Local Associates. The language for all reports and documentation is Portuguese.

Liaison with local municipality is in Portuguese and is entirely handled by the Local Associates, as RMJM staff have only a limited knowledge of the language.

One objective of the project is for the Local Associates to expand into architecture and engineering, so that provision is made for exchange of staff between RMJM and the local office for short periods.

Administration

Fees are paid locally in escudos, into a project joint account, released in an agreed proportion on client approval of each stage of work. RMJM's share is readily convertible to sterling. No ECGD cover has been taken out, being a project in the EC. Only the Local Associates pay local tax on their share: VAT on fees is paid by the client.

Main lessons

- As a first project in a new country it is advantageous not to set up a local firm or branch office, but form a joint venture agreement with a suitable local firm.
- The initial appraisal of the likely winning bid for fees and expenses and appropriate level of output was critical.
- In the event, more time by RMJM was needed than budgeted for, which reduced the project's profitability.

Case Study 11: Marine Science and Marine Resources Centre, Aden

Design and contract administration of a laboratory building for teaching and research in the marine sciences.

Location: Aden, Republic of Yemen
Client: Ministry of Fish Wealth
Value: $2 million
Funding: Islamic Development Bank (IDB)/UNESCO
Dates: Appointed 1987
              Handover 1990

Team

RMJM: Architects, Engineers, and Quantity Surveyors (pre-contract)
D G Jones & Partners: Quantity Surveyors (post-contract)

Business development

RMJM were selected by UNESCO (after shortlisting following completion of the Tripoli Museum in Libya).

Setting up

The project was carried out off-shore by RMJM & Partners as executive consultants. Although there were no local consultants or professional societies, foreign consultants were recognized and allowed to practise in the country. There were no foreign architects there when RMJM started work.

The client agreement was negotiated in Paris on the basis of a standard form produced by UNESCO, removing a number of potentially adverse clauses.

Appropriate design and technology

The climate is tropical hot-dry modified by maritime humidity, with high saline content. There are two monsoon seasons with high winds and abnormally high tides, and hence risks of flooding by sea-water. Steel reinforcement had to be protected, and all external metal components were either stainless steel or powder-coated aluminium, with special finishes to floors and walls vulnerable to sea-spray or overflow from sea-water installations. Special pipework, pumps and tanks were needed for sea-water service installations.

Stylistically the client preferred a modern international design. The local building industry's capability was limited to smaller local projects, and most materials and components had to be imported. There were no local planning or building regulations and British Codes of Practice, IEE Regulations, etc. were used throughout.

Implementation

Design, production and tender information was carried out in the UK, with periodic visits to Aden for client meetings. Tenders were sought from international firms in addition to the local building corporation (which, however, expressed reservations about constructing the engineering installations). A Chinese contractor (from the People's Republic) with imported Chinese labour, experienced in working in Aden, was appointed. The

Marine Science and Marine Resources Centre. Architects: RMJM (photo: RMJM).

contractor had English-speaking supervisors and translated all documentation into Chinese. The contractor's Aden office provided interpreters, but only one was experienced, so without him communications tended to be slow.

A delay of 18 months between inviting tenders and starting on site affected RMJM's fees and expenses (due to increases in salaries and air fares and adverse exchange rate fluctuations), for which compensating increases in charges for visits were negotiated. Periodic supervision was carried out mainly from RMJM's office in Dubai.

People

With no resident expatriate staff, or Local Associates, the project relied on the client initially to arrange visas, meetings, accommodation, etc.

Administration

Fees were paid direct in $ by UNESCO. Under the Agreement no local taxes were due to be paid: however, during the project a 5% tax was levied on RMJM's fees by the Yemeni tax authorities, on which an amicable agreement was eventually reached with the Ministry. The Agreement was subject to Yemeni law. ECGD cover was not taken out on the project, because of the agreement being with UNESCO.

During the contract the two republics of Yemen were unified, so that People's Democratic Republic of Yemen dinars and Yemen Arab Republic reals both circulated legally, leading to confusion.

There was no need for a Local Agent and the Ministry's project manager was very supportive in assisting with registrations (with the tax office and Chamber of Commerce), payment of tax, obtaining visas, immigration and exit procedures and cashing of travellers cheques. Initially visas took 2–3 weeks to obtain in the UK, but this became quicker and easier after the unification of the Yemen Arab Republic. Fee payments were held up because of delays in UNESCO receiving funds from IDB.

Main lessons

- This was a straightforward project executed by working off-shore.
- The Agreement needed careful negotiation, with legal advice.
- The effect of possible delays to the programme on fees and expenses needs to be covered in the client Agreement. Interest should be charged on late payments.
- With an international tender it is essential that the contractor's representatives are fluent English speakers, and that the contractor takes responsibility for translating all documentation into the language of his operatives.

Case Study 12: Saudi British Bank Buildings, Saudi Arabia

Design and contract administration of Headquarters building and three area branch banks for the Bank in Saudi Arabia.

Location: Headquarters and branch bank, Riyadh
                 Branch banks in Jeddah and Buraydah
Client: Saudi British Bank (SBB)
Value: £30 million
Funding: SBB
Dates: Appointed 1980
                 Construction start 1981
                 Completed 1984

Team

RMJM: Architects, Engineers, Landscape Architects, Quantity Surveyors (pre-contract)
Baker Wilkins & Smith: Quantity Surveyors (post-contract)
Consulting Architectural Corporation (CAC): Associate Architects

Business development

RMJM had been working in Saudi Arabia since 1970 (see Case Study 7) and were invited to carry out staff housing in Riyadh and Jeddah for the British Bank of the Middle East (BBME, RMJM's local bankers). As part of the process of conforming to the indigenization policy in Saudi Arabia, BBME changed its name to SBB and needed a new Headquarters and regional branch offices. RMJM were appointed on the basis of the success of their housing designs, which had been carried out in association with CAC (BBME's local architects).

Setting up

The status of architects as a profession is covered in Case Studies 3 and 7. By the date of this project a local Agent was required under Saudi law and a joint venture was set up of RMJM and Partners in association with CAC.

A joint venture Agreement was drawn up under which RMJM had the major design input, and CAC provided sponsorship, obtained visas and work permits, gave advice on the local building industry and materials, obtained planning and other

Saudi British Bank Building, Jeddah. Architects: RMJM (photo: RMJM).

approvals and took legal responsibility for staff. The joint
venture employed all site inspectorate staff (some on secondment
from RMJM in the UK) and shared profits on a sliding scale from
the design stage (where RMJM had the large majority) to contract
administration (where profits were split equally).

Appropriate design and technology

Saudi Arabia is a hot-dry mainly arid-desert country with shade
temperatures of over 50°C by day and night temperatures in
winter down to 10°C, and average annual rainfall of only 125 mm.
Jeddah's maritime climate is described in Case Study 7.

Being a Muslim country, where banking was introduced
relatively recently, the banks needed special facilities such as
separate rooms for clients to deposit large quantities of cash,
separate women's areas, and prayer spaces aligned to Mecca.
The client wanted the buildings to have a consistent corporate
style and a design that reflected Arab architecture. The design
adopted was based on the characteristic buildings of the desert
(where the majority of the buildings were located) with thick
limestone walls and narrow slit windows and large openings for
access well set back and shaded. This was also easier to air-
condition and more energy-efficient.

With the exception of aggregates and cement, all materials,
components and equipment were imported from countries
overseas. Main contractors were gradually changing from
Western companies to Middle Eastern or Saudi ones. Contractors
had difficulties in obtaining work permits for unskilled labour as
Saudis wished to limit immigration to people essential for
development of the nation.

Building control officers required a complete set of drawings
although they limited their review mainly to structure and
electrical installations (based on British or other international
standards) which had to be satisfied before a building permit
could be issued and thus before building work started. As will
be seen, this led to difficulties in practice.

Local fire-fighting standards conformed to American standards
(to local fire brigade approval), with means of escape and
sprinklers to British standards. There were no Saudi standards
for the building industry and thus British standards were used

(with American standards for car parking). Planning submissions were required much as in the UK, for consideration and approval by committees of nominated local people, advised by qualified planning staff.

Implementation

Briefing, client liaison and obtaining approvals took place in Saudi Arabia. Design, the preparation of production and tender information took place in the UK as the most economical and effective location. A standard design approach with marble cladding and bronze anodized windows was adopted for all the buildings to meet the client's wish for a corporate style.

The Riyadh branch bank went out to conventional selective tender, and the contract was won by a Cypriot company, J & P. Management contractors were interviewed for each of the Headquarters and remaining branch banks in order to overlap detail design and construction and permit changes of priority between buildings. The Laing/Wimpey/Ali Reza consortium was selected in each case.

The buildings were each divided into 12 standard packages for which tenders were obtained against an agreed estimate of prime cost. This caused difficulties in obtaining building permits, normally issued only after a completed set of working drawings had been submitted. Management contracting, which was new to Saudi Arabia, also ran into difficulties as the client representatives gradually changed from British to Saudi staff who were unfamiliar with the concept and tended to operate the contracts as conventional fixed-price building contracts.

A local office was established in Riyadh in 1981, when work started on the first site, to act as an office for liaison, contract administration and a base for site inspection. RMJM received excellent support from their Saudi Associates during both design and contract administration stages.

People

The RMJM team resident during the construction stage consisted of 12 professional staff and a Clerk of Works. The senior team members were posted with their families, and the remainder on bachelor status. One architect was resident in Jeddah: the remainder were accommodated in Riyadh in a residential compound comprising five villas and three apartments with a swimming pool, one of the villas being used as the liaison office.

Salaries and local taxation were as described in Case Study 3. Staff were provided by RMJM with accommodation, leave flights, fees for children's education, and cars. Local staff consisted of three secretaries, one bookkeeper, two drivers and a gardener.

A major incident arose when an expatriate member of the team was killed in a road accident 100 miles outside Riyadh. The project director had to identify and collect the body personally, arrange embalming at a local hospital and repatriation with personal effects to the UK. Although repatriation costs and death benefits to next of kin were covered by insurance, all other incidental costs, including mobilization of replacement staff, had to be covered within the lump-sum fee.

Administration

Fees up to contract were on a percentage basis, numerically below the UK level, but based on Saudi construction costs higher than the UK. Reduced fee levels for the branch banks were agreed on the grounds of repetition following the Headquarters building. However, the client changed the sequence of buildings to RMJM's disadvantage without accepting the effect on profitability. A lump-sum fee for the construction stage was agreed which more than adequately covered resident staff and associated costs already described.

There were no performance bonds or advance payment guarantees, since the client was from the private sector. No ECGD cover was taken out, due to the standing of the client and the country. The profitability of the project was enhanced by changes in the exchange rate during the life of the project working in RMJM's favour. All documentation on the project was in English, except for dealing with local authorities, which was carried out in Arabic by CAC.

RMJM's Professional Indemnity Policy in the UK not only covered RMJM's work without additional charge but also, at their request, was extended during the construction stage to CAC.

Main lessons

- It is essential to have a Local Associate/Agent whom you can work with and trust.
- The Saudi-ization of the client was not anticipated and led to changes and difficulties in programme and contract management.
- The fluctuation of the exchange rate worked in RMJM's favour.
- A good lump-sum fee negotiated for contract administration helped to offset the marginally profitable design and production information stage.
- The death of a team member had administrative and financial implications, which had not been foreseen.

Case Study 13: Ziu Zhou Hotel, Dalian, PRC

Design and contract administration of a 500-bed hotel in north-east China.

Location: Liaoning Province, People's Republic of China (PRC)
Client: Ziu Zhou JV Co/Holiday Inn
Value: $22 million
Funding: Private
Dates: Appointed 1987
              Completed 1990

Team

RMJM: Architects
Ove Arup and Partners: Structural and Services Engineers
Gammon Construction Ltd: Management Contractors
Dalian Institute of Engineers: Associate Architects

Business development

RMJM had been working in Hong Kong since 1965, and this opportunity to work in the PRC arose in discussion in Hong Kong with contractors and project managers. RMJM Hong Kong were appointed as consultants to the developer in Hong Kong who later selected a hotelier (Holiday Inn) and obtained financial backing from a bank in Hong Kong. The developer then set up a joint venture with a local Chinese developer, which became the principal client.

The Hong Kong member of the joint venture raised the equity, and the Chinese member provided the land and utilities. The whole development will pass to the Chinese members after 15–20 years: meanwhile the joint venture shares operating profits.

Setting up

The majority of work in the PRC is designed by the local Institutes of Engineers, with whom foreign consultants are required to work. Thus the local Dalian Institute became Local Associates with RMJM Hong Kong.

Appropriate design and technology

The site is in a marginal earthquake zone on the Yellow Sea between Peking and North Korea, about 1250 miles north of Hong Kong. The climate is similar to that of Scandinavia, hot in summer and very cold in winter, with low humidity and a wide diurnal temperature range in the spring and autumn.

In winter the hotel car park had to accommodate a high proportion of chauffeur-driven cars (for older local dignitaries who had never learnt to drive), resulting in a large waiting area and related mechanical ventilation. All hotels had to have basements to provide shelters against air raids. Many local people work part-time to spread the effects of high unemployment and overmanning is the norm; thus staff facilities had to be larger than normal.

There were no particular *Feng-shui* requirements for the site to be taken into account.

Stylistically the client wanted an international modern building (in keeping with the People's Republic's new status), but using local materials which were only technically suitable for low-rise buildings. The local building industry was mainly geared to unsophisticated low-rise buildings finished in ceramic tiles with no experience of the high-rise building needed by the

Ziu Zhou Hotel. Architects: RMJM (photo: RMJM).

client. Steel frame structure was virtually unknown, so a reinforced concrete frame was used, designed to be built through low winter temperatures. Construction methods were labour-intensive, especially below ground, and there was little off-site fabrication. For political and commercial reasons the local Joint Venture Associate was keen to use PRC-produced materials wherever possible – they were usually inappropriate.

Working hours were short in winter, and cold-climate construction methods, though relatively crude, were effective.

Building workers (often itinerant) lived in the buildings under construction which affected trade sequences and partial hand-over. Heating of buildings was normally by low-grade coal, which polluted the atmosphere and attacked external surfaces. In the absence of normal cleaning, the building was designed for low maintenance.

Local planning regulations were simple (i.e. building line, plot-ratio, and use) but agreement by the local committee was the result of highly democratic and unhurried circular debate – usually in a restaurant (the only available large space). Fire fighting and means of escape were designed to known international standards, as local regulations did not cover multi-storey hotels.

Local building regulations were rather obscure and open to interpretation (except for basic structural stability). For building standards we followed the procedures in the Hong Kong office (as most materials would be ordered and imported through Hong Kong). High-risk materials (mainly in the external skin) were specified to be obtained from Europe, under BS and DIN standards, since these were the ones we were familiar with. For lower-risk items (e.g. sanitary-ware) we widened the specification to accept US or Japanese standards.

Implementation

A very fast start was required to get building under way within six months from commissioning before the winter weather closed the site. All work up to the tender was carried out in Hong Kong by a team composed of British expatriate and bilingual Mandarin/English-speaking Hong Kong architects for speed and economy and ease of liaison with the principal client and hotelier. There were periodic visits to Dalian for planning presentations and liaison with the local Institute of Engineers. Extensive presentations were required with bilingual titles and annotation to drawings, given by Mandarin-speaking architects from the team.

A shortlist of pre-qualified Chinese contractors drawn from the People's Republic submitted tenders on a simple Bill of Quantities and schedule of rates. The final choice of contractor was the result of negotiation by the local Joint Venture Associate.

A similar process for international mechanical and electrical sub-contractors resulted in a choice of a Japanese firm.

Supervision was based in the Hong Kong office, but with resident engineer and architect living in Dalian, recruited in Hong Kong, with a telex link to Hong Kong.

People

The key members of staff locally were the resident engineer and resident architect, already mentioned. They were paid two to three times their equivalent salary in Hong Kong to compensate for the very poor living conditions in Dalian, and the pressures put on them by the local Chinese. They were at the beck and call of local officials seven days a week, and frequently pressurized into reducing their leave periods in Hong Kong. Alternatively, when temporary replacements were sent out to cover holiday periods their return was resisted if they were preferred to the resident staff member!

Administration

The fee agreement was basically a lump sum tied to the project funding paid in HKD to RMJM as lead consultant in Hong Kong, in three stages up to tender, and monthly in equal payments during contract. In the event, this led to an acute cash flow problem, as planning permission (which triggered the first stage payment) was not obtained until the tender stage. Thereafter interest was negotiated (and paid) on all overdue fee payments, to minimize delay. At about 6% for all skills for a full service this represented very good value for money for the client, but was not very profitable for the consultants. No local taxation was payable either by RMJM or local professional staff.

Main lessons

- It is difficult to do a good professional job in the People's Republic. China is not a golden rice bowl.

- It is crucial to include timely fee payments in the project finance package.
- In dealing with the PRC team RMJM's project director had to rely more on personal relationships and trust than on contracts and paper.

Case Study 14: Moscow Golf and Country Club, Russia

Design of a 250-room 5-star hotel, Leisure Centre and 18-hole golf course on a site in Moscow.

Location: On the outskirts of Moscow, Russia
Client: Sovengo: Soviet/British joint venture with Golf Shows Ltd
Value: Approx. £50 million
Funding: Private
Dates: Appointed 1987
Started on site 1991

Team

RMJM: Architects, Engineers, Landscape Architects
Golf-Consult: Golf Course Architects
Ash Preston & Partners: Quantity Surveyors
Simon Carves: Project Managers/Contractors

Business development

With the sudden opening up of the USSR through *perestroika*, the country became a potential market for projects, wherever they could be funded in hard currency. Through membership of BCB, RMJM was invited by Golf Shows Ltd to produce an outline building concept, in competition with foreign consortia from Germany, Japan, South Korea, Sweden and the USA. After selection a letter of intent was initialled by Golf Shows Ltd and Sovintersport (a company sponsored by the Soviet Sports Ministry) to form a joint venture, Sovengo, which was eventually signed a year later.

Setting up

When work started all Soviet architects were employed by the state, and the concept of an independent profession was unknown. RMJM's work has been entirely off-shore with considerable advice and cooperation from architects/engineers of the Sports Ministry and Mossoviet, with short visits to Moscow for presentations. It was important not to oversell skills and experience, but to focus on the development of an atmosphere of trust.

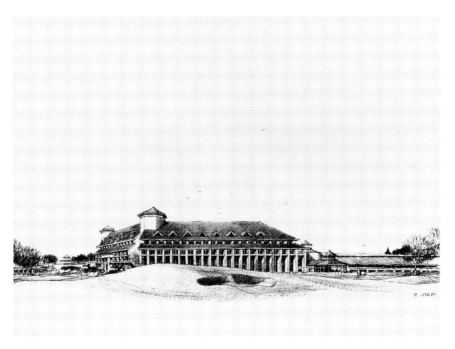

Moscow Golf and Country Club. Architects: RMJM (sketch: RMJM).

Appropriate design and technology

The prevailing climate varies between extremes of heat and cold (+30°C to −20°C), with snow for half the year. All materials and components have to be imported, with the possible exception of aggregates, cement and steel reinforcement.

There is a local tradition of fabricating large structural elements in reinforced concrete in factories during the cold months, for rapid erection and enclosure of buildings during the hot months, but the state-controlled building industry is not an appropriate organization to respond to the need for fixed deliveries, prices and alternative forms of construction. The brief eventually specified the adoption of a traditional British style architecture, since the building is mainly for use by foreigners resident in, and visiting, Moscow and paying for services in hard currency.

As the project developed the evolving "democracy" recognized the need for three tiers of approval to acquire and develop land: the Trade Union of the Ministry of Sport, Moscow City Council, and the Local District Council. Building standards were initially based on Canadian and British codes, and subsequently on Soviet codes once they had been obtained and translated. The Soviet half of the Sovengo joint venture proved invaluable partners in their ability to procure approvals and guide the architect.

Implementation

Over a period of 2 years RMJM developed the design sufficiently to obtain planning permission and technical approvals to the building. In parallel, the client sought and involved the hotel operator and raised equity from private investment funds, the hotel operator, and a major UK bank for debt finance.

Though often delayed, the project has remained alive in the rapidly changing scene in the former USSR. Construction finally began in June 1991 with a Russian company responsible for the infrastructure and ground works, only to be suspended when the country's constitution changed.

People

The project has needed senior people with the flexibility and imagination to cope with an environment which needs new systems tailored to an innovative commercial construction contract and the ability to communicate design ideas simply.

Administration

This is a hard-currency contract dependent on external investment, with the Russian counterparts producing non-convertible roubles to pay for costs of land, and local labour and materials.

Main lessons

- This is an interesting case of a project in a country with vast resources undergoing a fundamental and rapid change in its political and economic status.
- The project has been subjected to several stops and starts through changes in investor confidence in the changing political scene: but the joint Russian/British team, who had established a totally trusting working relationship from the inception, were able to keep it alive. The Russian authorities and counterparts in the joint venture have proved reliable in all their dealings, and extremely able collaborators.

Case Study 15: Happy Valley Racecourse Grandstands, Hong Kong

Design and contract administration of the rebuilding and refurbishment of the grandstands at Happy Valley Racecourse.

Location: Hong Kong
Client: Royal Hong Kong Jockey Club (RHKJC)
Cost: £36 million
Funding: RHKJC
Dates: Appointed 1986
              Completed 1990

Team

RMJM Hong Kong Limited: Architects and Interior Designers
Ove Arup & Partners: Civil, Structural and M&E Engineers
Levett & Bailey: Quantity Surveyors
Trett Wardale: Programming Consultants
RHKJC: Project Manager

Business development

RMJM have been established in Hong Kong since 1981 following appointments for projects for China Light & Power and the Hong Kong Government. While developing a client base for specialist building design, the company's first appointment with RHKJC was in 1983 for the design of the Equine Hospital to service over 600 racehorses stabled by the Club. Further commissions followed and in 1986 the company was appointed as lead consultant for the major rebuilding and refurbishment of public and members' grandstand facilities at the Club's city-centre racecourse in Happy Valley on Hong Kong Island.

Setting up

The Hong Kong Institute of Architects (HKIA) is the governing architectural authority in Hong Kong and is well established with professional members. Its terms of reference for architects' appointments, scope of service and fee structures are a much simplified version of the RIBA's *Architect's appointment*. Since the beginning of 1991, the HK Government has introduced the Architects Registration Ordinance which requires all architects to register with the Architects Registration Board before they may practise under the title of "Architect" in Hong Kong. Registration requires either previous membership of HKIA for automatic registration or passing an examination board.

Happy Valley Racecourse Grandstands. Architects: RMJM (photo: RMJM).

Building control is via the Town Planning Board, District Lands Office and the Buildings Ordinance Office (BOO) of the HK Government which enforces the building regulations. Design and construction submissions to BOO must be made by Authorized Persons (architects, engineers or surveyors) who have passed the relevant BOO examination for technical competence and knowledge of the Building Ordinances and Regulations. Submission procedures are complex and rigidly controlled by BOO. Approval of drawings and calculations indicating compliance with regulations and consent for commencement of construction work must be obtained throughout the entire design and construction process, which culminates in inspection by the Fire Services Department, Water Authority and BOO before achieving an Occupation Permit for the completed development.

All consultants were independently appointed by the client and RMJM were appointed as lead consultants working with the Club's in-house project management team which was part of the Property Department. RMJM were, as part of their services, required to act as Authorized Person and be responsible for the BOO submissions and approvals procedures. Appointment was by letter confirming the percentage fee scale to be used.

At appointment our office in Hong Kong numbered about 30 staff, about a third of whom were expatriates and two-thirds Hong Kong Chinese.

Appropriate design and technology

The climate is tropical, hot and humid, up to 95% RH in the summer. Rainfall is up to 3 m per annum, mostly falling between May and September.

Although protected by its location on the north side of the island in a valley, the site is vulnerable to the annual typhoons so that design had to comply with the Hong Kong Code of Practice on wind effects. Uplift and negative pressures on roofs, windows and cladding are often more onerous than dead loads.

The building is of considerable local significance as horse-racing provides the only legalized form of betting, which itself is a major Chinese pastime. The brief was to increase the facilities for betting and catering by 50%, and improve views of the racetrack, while maintaining a minimum level of betting activity during rebuilding. A limitation of the design (to conform to the *Feng-shui* of the site) was that no windows were allowed to face the cemetery on the other side of the adjoining street.

See Case Study 1 for comments on architectural style, planning and building regulations and the resources of the local building industry. The accent is on speed of construction and rapid pay-back on buildings. Long delivery periods of components from overseas (mostly the USA and Europe) may exclude their use in favour of locally manufactured components, even if of lower quality.

Project implementation

The restricted programme imposed by keeping racing going required construction to start within 6 months of the design team's appointment, and separate tendering for each of the four phases of work. A cost plan based on early sketch drawings was used as the basis of cost control. The design team worked in close collaboration with five separate client departments (betting, racing, property, catering and membership) to coordinate their disparate requirements.

Priority status was sought from, and granted by, BOO to facilitate rapid approval and consent procedures. An exemption from the Buildings Ordinance was also obtained for cantilevering fire escape stairs and service ducts over the adjacent street. The entire project relied on first-time approvals, with no float in the programme. Licensing and government approvals were essential to enable the racing to take place on the appointed day. Mock-ups of new betting facilities were built, delivered and modified to ensure total compliance with client requirements before multiple modules were constructed.

Fast-track programming, tendering on Bills of (approximate) Quantities, and client purchasing of long-delivery items were necessary to fit into the racing calendar, and ensure completion of each stage of work by the date of the first race meeting. Tenderers for the General Contract and major sub-contracts were local firms, prequalified on the basis of their demonstrated ability to perform under such rigorous conditions. Selection was by competitive tender.

A design team office was established on site and a full team of architectural, structural and services site inspectorate staff was provided to ensure compliance with contract documentation, resolve site queries without delay, and maintain quality control. All four phases of work were duly completed and received government approvals and operating licences on time.

People

All members of the design team had worked with the RHKJC before and were experienced in meeting the demands of the client and aware of the necessity to complete on time. Senior expatriate RMJM staff managed the project at all stages, with local technical back-up.

Resident RMJM Directors and Associates were seconded from the UK on a family posting with a salary mark-up of about 30%, plus an annual return air fare to the UK, furnished accommodation, and car provided by the firm. Individual taxation was up to 15% of gross salary paid up to a year in arrears. There was no PAYE or NI and accommodation provided by RMJM was taxed to a total of 10% of total earnings. There was no Double Taxation Agreement with the UK.

Administration

See Case Study 1. There was no ECGD cover as the project was carried out by our Hong Kong company. Our company was subject to Hong Kong corporation tax on profits of 16%, and operates under Hong Kong law and ordinances.

Main lessons

- A seemingly impossible programme was achieved by co-operation between client, design team and contractor (together with extremely high liquidated and ascertained damages clauses).
- This achievement was made possible by the common attitude

of all participants to working hard and effectively, which is a characteristic of the business climate in Hong Kong.

- Our part of this work as architects and lead consultants was critical and was achieved by careful choice of senior staff with wide experience of work in Hong Kong, and skilled support by local staff in the office and on site.

Appendix A: Costing Overseas Submissions

I Sequence

RMJM's experience suggests that you should proceed in the following sequence.

1. Attempt to produce a full build-up of estimated costs using standard headings in Section II with supporting schedules. Do not use "emergency kit" methods unless there is no alternative because of shortage of time.
2. Attempt to obtain agreement of client to a fee with separate reimbursement of expenses and capital items at cost plus 10% handling charge. (The capital items should be treated as returnable at the end of the project.)
3. Make a best estimate of technical man-months, including the leave and down-time in those man-months. (Allow 6 weeks leave p.a. but no terminal leave or end-of-job bonuses.) Carefully assess the appropriate service to be given, with no "over-cooking". Include for mobilizing and closing down.
4. Decide for each costing category what contingency margin to add and whether a profit should be added. Probably a profit should be taken only on salaries, salary-related costs and overheads and not on reimbursable or capital items. A 10–15% contingency should be added in lump-sum bids.
5. Decide what "life-style" is necessary or possible, e.g. who will be resident with wife and family. These should probably be limited to the Project Director, and possibly the Deputy Project Director – all

the others being on bachelor status with 10-week tours and 2 weeks back in the UK – although true bachelors may only have local leave. It is better to pay well and reduce other benefits in kind if a competitive edge is to be maintained.

6. The costing accountant should show clearly in backup papers what assumptions, margins, contingencies and profit percentages (and any special loading factors) have been added so that the negotiator can assess the implications of coming down in negotiation in so many percentage stages. Some indication of the real lowest bid "cut-off" point should be given. Directors' time should be shown and a separate fee put in, but no other contingencies or profit margins added to the fee. If a purely "negotiating margin" has been added this should be made clear, so that the best estimate of cost is separate from the "preliminaries".

7. If there is the possible alternative of doing part of the work in a different geographical location more cheaply this should be shown and costed.

8. Prepare a project cash flow chart in order to establish and justify advance payments needed, and to show the effect of any known restriction on remittances of fees earned in the country.

9. Assess the risks of failure of other members of a consortium to perform their part of the work, and thus delay you doing, or getting paid for, your work. Ideally the project should be packaged so that your work is as self-sufficient as possible.

10. Check levels of building costs and predictions of inflation in the country before deciding on the level of scale fees to accept.

11. Assess the level of pre-contract costs to be covered by the fees, both for yourself and other team members (including your Local Associates) and ensure that the negotiator knows where they are included.

12. The negotiator should go over the main characteristics, assumptions and negotiating strategy on significant projects in the office – especially to get "political" guidance and backing on how low to go finally if pushed hard.

13. The negotiator should be given the responsibility of deciding whether to sign the final agreement or not. It is best for him to be the prospective director in charge and that he is accompanied by a second director when possible.

If one of the resident wives is a good secretary, with no children and some nursing experience, and a valid driving licence, you will indeed have a lucky bonus!

At the fee-negotiating stage on MDA-funded projects, the prospective client will have from the Bank a guide calculation to man-month costing rates adjusted for the particular conditions. It is important to arrange your calculations in the same way and under the same headings so that misleading comparisons are not made to your disadvantage.

II Typical headings

A. Sterling costs

A1 Remuneration of professional services

Built up as a schedule of team members with number of man-months × charging rates.

A2 Reimbursable expenses

- Mobilization, demobilization:
  - Number of return trips built up by team members and families.
  - Home-country inland travel: number of trips × unit rates.
  - Visa, health and travel documents: number of trips × unit rates.
  - Return air fares: number of trips by destination × unit rates.
  - Excess baggage: number of trips × unit rates.
  - Freight of company and personal goods.
  - En-route *per diem* international travel stop-over: number of trips × unit rates.
  - Hotels on arrival and departure: number of trips × unit rates.

- Books (including air freighting).
- Communications at home office (including telephone, cable, telex, fax, postage and courier): months × lump sum rate.
- Special surveys, models, computer work, etc.

A3 Handling charge: A2 × 10%

A4 Sub-total (A1 + A2 + A3)

A5 Contingencies A4 × (10–15%)

A6 Total in £

B. Local costs (in local currency)

B1 Remuneration of professional services

Built up as A1

B2 Reimbursable expenses

- Mobilization and demobilization: visa, work permits, etc.: number of trips × unit rate.
- Subsistence (per diem): days × unit rate.
- Accommodation:
  - Housing and related costs: number × unit rate.
  - Hotel accommodation for foreign consultants: number of nights × unit rate.
- School fees: number × unit rate.
- Medical costs: months × unit costs.
- Office accommodation:
  - Rental: team number × 10 m² × months × unit rate.
  - Equipment: schedule of items and costs.
  - Running costs (to cover power, light, consumables, communications): lump sum months × unit rate.
- Insurance: monthly rate.
- Drawing office materials: months × unit rate.
- Reports and document reproduction: numbers × unit cost.
- Local staff: schedule with number of man-months × rate.
- Local transportation:
  - cars: number × unit cost.
  - hotel/office/meetings: foreign consultant man-days × unit cost.
  - office/client/local authority, etc.: number of days × unit cost.
- Site visits:
  - transportation: days × unit costs
  - hotel accommodation: nights × unit costs
  - subsistence: days × unit costs
  - equipment hire.
- Taxes and duties.
- Closing-down costs:
  - terminating local staff contracts.
  - disposal of office, housing, furniture and equipment.
  - disposal of files and drawings.
  - disposal of cars.
  - obtaining final fee payment.
  - completion of accounts and final tax-clearance certificates.

B3 Handling charge: B2 × 10%

B4 Sub-total (B1 + B2 + B3)

B5 Contingencies B4 × (10–15%)

B6 Total (in local currency)

III Typical breakdown of time-based rates for expatriate staff

A. Basic salary (per unit of chargeable time)

B. UK social charges (20% short-term dropping to 15% long term) × A including:

- National Social Security
- Pension and life insurance
- Public holiday and sick leave
- Annual leave
- Car
- Travel insurance
- Kit allowance.

C. Overheads (150% short-term dropping to 15% long term) × A home office-based expenses including:

- Office expenses
- Office running expenses
- Motor expenses
- Administrative and secretarial staff
- Legal, audit and bank charges
- Standing time
- Job getting and closing
- Insurance, finance, etc.

D. Fee: 15% × (A+B+C)
Risks, capital servicing, reserves and profit

E. Overseas allowance: 20–80% × A

F. Allowance for withholding tax 25% × (A+B+C+D+E)

G. Charging rate (A+B+C+D+E+F)

H. Multiplier (G÷A)

IV Conditions

A. Period of acceptance

B. Period for rates to hold firm and method for updating

C. Method of payment:

- Periodic payment of fees: method of calculation.
- Mobilization fee as percentage of total fee.
- Payment of reimbursable expenses monthly, preferably as lump sum (which is administratively much easier) otherwise supported by evidence of actual expenditure.
- Period of payment.
- Interest of overdue fees and expenses.
- Location of payment of sterling and local currency respectively.

D. Assumptions on local tax covering:

- Stamp duty on contract
- Sales tax
- Withholding tax
- Road tax
- VAT.

Appendix B: Checklist of Heads of Agreement in Individual Staff Contracts

1. The parties, etc
   Date of agreement; name and address of firm; name and address of employee; preamble referring to client, project, country, etc.

2. The employment
   Starting date, location of post; time and place for reporting for duty; scope, occupation, position held, title, grade; secondment, take instructions from, responsible to; introductory period in UK, length of tour, probationary period; extensions, number of tours; transfers; uniform.

3. Remuneration
   See Annex at the end of this appendix for categories of remuneration or reimbursement.

4. Travel and freight-rate for personal effects
   Fares paid; class, frequency, excess baggage cost and freightage (including household effects); removal, package, insurance, delivery costs; passports, visas, work permits, customs formalities, local travel; fares, car insurance, fuel, maintenance, driver.

5. Passages for family
   Outward and return journeys (including on death of employee overseas); holiday passages to UK; children's school journeys; travel to UK on compassionate grounds. Equivalent flights on "bachelor" posting.

6. Quarters
   Sale or rental of house in UK (including legal and other fees); expenses; settling-in period, hotel allowances (including family)

while finding quarters; rent-free quarters (including standard of quality), rates, gas, electricity, water and telephone (occupy and deliver up); contributions towards rental and costs of quarters; list of hard furnishings, bedding, air conditioners/heaters supplied free; list of items to be supplied by employer (e.g. cutlery, crockery, kitchenware, TV/radio, soft furnishing); laundry, cook, house-keeper, servant, gardener, insurances.

7. Hours and leave
Working day, week, overtime, local leave and public holidays; UK home leave; terminal leave (end of tour) or pay in lieu; carry forward arrangements, sick leave, compassionate leave, repatriation leave, fares to recognised holiday centre.

8. Arrangement when on local tour
Reimbursable expenses for travel, accommodation, subsistence, laundry, second car for family.

9. Insurances and pensions
Payment of NI (overseas rates excluding industrial injury); insurance, life, accident, travel, sickness, disability (loss of limbs, etc.), repatriation due to sickness, local medical expenses, cost of emergency travel, BUPA/PPP, public liability, etc.; pensions scheme; retirement, age, payments; PI insurance (including waiver of prorogation).

10. Inability to perform duties
Sickness: certificates, payment during sickness (less NI benefits); pay if taken hostage, etc.

11. Suspension, dismissal and termination
Reasons for suspension, reinstatement, dismissal without notice (e.g. breach of contract, neglect, absence without leave, wilful neglect/injury, etc.); termination; period of notice, *force majeure*, penalties for premature termination, address for notice.

12. Repatriation rights
Fares, see 4 and 5 above; leave, see 7 above; sickness, see 9 above; resettlement (upheaval) allowance, redundancy pay, house purchase, storage costs, etc.

13. Professional conduct
Secrecy and security; serve to best ability, using care, skill, etc.; exclusivity, no private practice; be bound by code of professional conduct (state which); disclosure of inventions, interest, copyright, patents, registered designs, trademarks, publicity, press, radio, TV; contracting with third parties; firm's regulations; employee debts.

14. Legal provisions
    Changes in terms of agreement and service; disputes, arbitration; interpretation by law of England or other country; jurisdiction of English courts; definitions (e.g. what constitutes "overseas", "tour of duty").

    Signatures: for Firm, Employee, Witnesses.

Annex: Categories of remuneration or reimbursement

- Basic salary (and pay, if any, for overtime working).
- Frequency, payment in arrears.
- Bonus, profit share, incentive payments.
- Currency, place, bank for payment.
- Allowances for:
  Length of tour (i.e. disturbance, separation): climate/amenities (congeniality): cost of living (if above UK level): level of responsibility.
- Local taxes, NI, imports, import duties, etc.
- Tax adjustment (including cost of accountant's advice).
- Exchange control restrictions.
- Devaluation of currency.
- Loss/gain on currency conversion; convertibility.
- Education/schooling expenses locally or in UK.
- Allowances for:
  Settling in; special kit (tropical/winter); entertaining; club entrance and subscriptions (including family); language training (including spouse).
- Review period/inflation/indexation to local cost of living.
- Redundancy pay.
- Pay in lieu of leave.
- Resettlement costs in UK.
- Terminal gratuity.

Appendix C: Glossary of Acronyms

ACE	Architects Council for Europe
	also Association of Consulting Engineers
AFNOR	Association Française de Normalisation
AIA	The American Institute of Architects
AIDS	Acquired Immune Deficiency Syndrome
ARCUK	Architects Registration Council of the United Kingdom
ATP-TC	Aid and Trade Provision – Technical Cooperation
BCB	British Consultants Bureau
BILD	Building Insurance against Latent Defects
BRE	Building Research Establishment
BS	British Standard
BSI	British Standards Institution
BSRIA	Building Services Research and Information Association
CAA	Commonwealth Association of Architects
CCMI	Centre for Construction Market Information
CEN	Comité Européen des Normalisation
CIMA	Chartered Institute of Management Accountants
CIRIA	Construction Industry Research and Information Association
CIS	Commonwealth of Independent States (formerly the USSR)
COMET	Committee for Middle East Trade
CV	Curriculum vitae
DACON	Data on Consultants Form
DIN	Deutsches Institut für Normung
DOE	Department of the Environment
DTI	Department of Trade and Industry
EC	European Community
ECA	Economic Conditions Abroad Ltd
ECGD	Export Credit Guarantee Department
ECIS	European Council of International Schools

EEIG	European Economic Interest Grouping
EFCA	European Federation of Engineering Consultancy Associations
EFTA	European Free Trade Area
EGCI	Export Group for the Construction Industries
ETA	European Technical Assessment
FCO	Foreign and Commonwealth Office
FIDIC	Fédération Internationale des Ingénieurs-Conseils
GLC	Greater London Council
GNP	Gross National Product
HMG	Her Majesty's Government
HMSO	Her Majesty's Stationery Office
ICC	International Chamber of Commerce
IUA	International Union of Architects
JIS	Japanese Industry Standard
LCCI	London Chamber of Commerce and Industry
MASTA	Medical Advisory Service for Travellers Abroad
MDA	Multilateral Development Agency
N&D	Norman & Dawbarn
NEDC	National Economic Development Council
ODA	Overseas Development Administration
OECD	The Organization for Economic Cooperation and Development.
OECF	Overseas Economic Co-operation Fund (The Japanese equivalent of ODA)
OPF	Overseas Project Fund
PAM	Pertubuhan Akitek Malaysia
PEP	Project and Exports Policy Division (of DTI)
PI	Professional Indemnity
PRC	The People's Republic of China
REDR	Registered Engineers for Disaster Relief
RIBA	The Royal Institute of British Architects
RMJM	formerly Robert Matthew Johnson-Marshall and Partners
SBB	Saudi British Bank
SEATAG	South-east Asia Trade Advisory Group
THE	Technical Help to Exporters
UK	United Kingdom
UN	United Nations
UNESCAP	United Nations Economic and Social Commission for Asia and the Pacific
UNESCO	United Nations Educational, Scientific and Cultural Organization
USA	United States of America
USAID	United States Aid
VSO	Voluntary Services Overseas

Appendix D: Contact Addresses

(all in UK unless otherwise indicated)

The American Institute of Architects
1735 New York Avenue NW
Washington DC 20006
USA

Tel: (202) 626 7300

The Association of Language-Export Centres
PO Box 1574
London NW1 4NJ

Tel: 071 224 3748
Fax: 071 224 3518

Barclays Bank plc
PO Box 12
Barclays House
1 Wimborne Road
Poole
Dorset BH15 2BB

Tel: 0202 671212
Fax: 0202 402098

British Consultants Bureau
1 Westminster Palace Gardens
1/9 Artillery Row
London SW1P 1RJ

Tel: 071 222 3651
Fax: 071 222 3664

The British Council
10 Spring Gardens
London SW1A 2BN

Tel: 071 930 8466
Fax: 071 839 6347

The British Embassy
3100 Massachusetts Avenue
Washington DC 20008
USA

Tel: (202) 898 4456
Fax: (020) 898 4255

Building Research Establishment
Garston
Watford WD2 7JR

Tel: 0923 894040
Fax: 0923 664010

Building Services Research and Information Association
Eurocentre
Old Bracknell Lane West
Bracknell
Berkshire RG12 4AH

Tel: 0344 426511
Fax: 0344 487575

Business International Ltd
40 Duke Street
London W1A 1DW

Tel: 071 493 6711
Fax: 071 499 9767

Centre for Construction Market Information
26 Store Street
London WC1E 7BT

Tel: 071 580 4949
Fax: 071 631 0329

The Centre for International Briefing
Farnham Castle
Farnham
Surrey GU9 0AG

Tel: 0252 721194
Fax: 0252 711283

Commission of the European Communities
8 Storey's Gate
London SW1P 3AT

Tel: 071 973 1992

Construction Industry Research and Information Association
6 Storey's Gate
Westminster
London SW1P 3AU

Tel: 071 222 8891
Fax: 071 222 1708

De Pinna Scorers & John Venn
3 Albermarle Street
London W1X 3HF

Tel: 071 409 3188
Fax: 071 491 7302

DOE
2 Marsham Street
London SW1P 3EB
● Single European Market Branch
  Construction Market Division

Tel: 071 276 3146
Fax: 071 276 3826

DTI
See Overseas Trade Services below

Dun and Bradstreet Ltd
Holmers Farm Way
High Wycombe
Bucks HP12 4UL

Tel: 0494 422000
Fax: 0494 422260

Economic Conditions Abroad Ltd
Anchor House
15 Britten Street   Tel: 071 351 7151
London SW3 3TY   Fax: 071 351 9396

European Bank of Reconstruction and Development
122 Leadenhall Street   Tel: 071 338 6000
London EC3V 4EB   Fax: 071 338 6100

European Council of International Schools
21B Lavant Street
Petersfield   Tel: 0730 68244
Hants GU23 3EL   Fax: 0730 67914

Export Credit Guarantee Department
2 Exchange Tower
Harbour Exchange Square   Tel: 071 512 7000
London E14 9GS   Fax: 071 512 7649

Export Group for the Construction Industries
Kingsbury House
15–17 King Street
St James's   Tel: 071 930 5377
London SW1Y 6QU   Fax: 071 930 2306

Export Opportunities Ltd
Export House
87A Wembley Hill Road
Wembley   Tel: 081 900 1313
Middlesex HA9 8BU   Fax: 081 900 1268

Fédération Internationale des Ingénieurs-Conseils
PO Box 86
1000 Lausanne 12   Tel: (21) 6535003
Switzerland   Fax: (21) 6535432

The Institute of Linguists
24a Highbury Grove   Tel: 071 359 7445
London N5 2EA   Fax: 071 354 0202

International Chamber of Commerce (United Kingdom)
14–15 Belgrave Square   Tel: 071 823 2811
London SW1X 8PS   Tel: 071 235 5447

International Union of Architects
51 rue Raynouard
75016 Paris   Tel: (1) 4524 3688
France   Fax: (1) 4524 0278

The Law Society
Legal Practice Directorate (International)
50/52 Chancery Lane   Tel: 071 320 5776
London WC2A 1SX   Fax: 071 831 0057

London Chamber of Commerce and Industry
69 Cannon Street   Tel: 071 248 4444
London EC4N 5AB   Fax: 071 489 0391

London School of Hygiene and Tropical Medicine
Keppel Street   Tel: 071 634 4408
London WC1E 7HT   Fax: 071 323 4547

The Meteorological Office
Overseas Climatology Division
Johnson House
London Road
Bracknell   Tel: 0344 855937
Berkshire RG12 2SY   Fax: 0344 854906

National Economic Development Office
Millbank Tower
Millbank   Tel: 071 217 4000
London SW1P 4QX   Fax: 071 821 1099

OMTRAC
Linford House
44 Linford Street   Tel: 071 738 8218
London SW8 4UN   Fax: 071 627 3398

Overseas Development Administration

- Consultancies Section
  Abercombie House
  Eaglesham Road
  East Kilbride   Tel: 0355 844000
  Glasgow G75 8EA   Fax: 0355 844099

- Information Department
  94 Victoria Street   Tel: 071 917 0503
  London SW1E 5JL   Fax: 071 917 0502

Overseas Economic Cooperation Fund
9–15 Sackville Street   Tel: 071 434 3211
London W1X 1DE   Fax: 071 494 3066

Overseas Trade Services
Joint Directorate
DTI and Foreign & Commonwealth Office
1–19 Victoria Street   Tel: 071 215 5000
London SW1H 0ET   Fax: 071 222 2629

- European Single Market Hotline   Tel: 081 200 1992
- World Aid Section
  123 Victoria Street   Tel: 071 215 6512
  London SW1E 6RB   Fax: 071 215 6535

Registered Engineers for Disaster Relief
1–7 Great George Street   Tel: 071 233 3116
London SW1P 3AA   Fax: 071 222 7500

The Royal Institute of British Architects
66 Portland Place   Tel: 071 580 5533
London W1N 4AD   Fax: 071 255 1541

- Competitions Office
  8 Woodhouse Square   Tel: 0532 456250
  Leeds LS3 1AD   Fax: 0532 426791

Technical Help to Exporters
BSI
Linford Wood   Tel: 0908 220022
Milton Keynes MK14 6LE   Fax: 0908 320856

Thomas Telford Ltd
Thomas Telford House
1 Heron Quay   Tel: 071 987 6999
London E14 9XF   Fax: 071 538 4101

Voluntary Services Overseas Ltd
317 Putney Bridge Road   Tel: 081 780 2266
London SW15 2PN   Fax: 081 780 1326

Women's Corona Society
Commonwealth House
18 Northumberland Avenue   Tel: 071 839 7908
London WC2N 5BJ

The World Bank
1818 H Street NW   Tel: (202) 477 1234
Washington DC 20433   Fax: (202) 477 6391
USA

Appendix E: Bibliography

1. Background

(a) General

Francis Baden-Powell: *Encyclopedia of Architecture*, article on International Practice: John Wiley & Sons Inc, New York 1989.

T Bidgood: *Future Markets for Consultancy*: Northwood Publications, London 1980 (op).

V L Cox: *International Construction, Marketing, Planning and Execution*: Longman Press, London 1982 (op).

R Cunliffe: "The lessons from working abroad", *The Architects' Journal* **171**(7), 351–356 (13 February 1980).

A Konya: "Architecture for export", *The Architects' Journal* **168** (34, 35 & 36), 318–351, 391–403, 406–443 (23 & 30 August, 6 September 1978).

(b) Design

M Evans: *Housing, Climate and Comfort*: Architectural Press, London 1980 (op).

M Fry and J Drew: *Tropical Architecture in the Dry and Humid Zones*: Krieger, New York 1975.

O H Koenigsberger, *et al*: *Manual of Tropical Housing*, Part 1 *Climate Design*: Longman Press, London 1974 (op).

R Matthew, S Johnson-Marshall, *et al*: *Standards Guide for Universities*: National Universities Commission, Lagos 1978.

V Olgyay: *Design with Climate, Bioclimatic Approach to Architectural Regionalism*: Princeton University Press, Princeton NJ 1963.

YRM International: *Health Buildings in Hot Climates, Design Guide for Thermal Performance*: DHSS London 1976 (op).

(c)   Administration
   J Arkell: Overseas Contracts Seminar; Paper on *Finance, Insurance, Tax and Law*: The Institution of Civil Engineers, London 1979.
   Francis Baden-Powell: the *Ivanhoe Guide to Chartered Architects*, article on *Working Overseas*: the Ivanhoe Press, Oxford 1990.
   B M Shephard: *How to Set up a Company Anywhere in the European Community*: Birmingham Publishing Co., Birmingham 1990.

2. References in text

1 *World Development Report 1991: The Challenge of Development*: World Bank, Washington 1991.
2 Weld Coxe: *Marketing Architectural and Engineering Services*: Van Nostrand Rheinhold, New York 1983.
3 *Notes on Guidance for the Exporting Consultant*: BCB, London 1991.
4 *British Overseas Aid: Opportunities for Business*: ODA, London 1989.
5 Warren Baum: *The Project Cycle*: The World Bank, Washington 1982.
6 J M Coates and B J Williamson: *The International Consultant's Manual: a Guide to Winning Consultancy Assignments*: Aedilis Book Co., Hong Kong 1991.
7 *Guidelines for the Use of Consultants by World Bank Borrowers and by the World Bank as Executing Agency*: World Bank, Washington, DC 1981.
8 *A Guide to Gaining Business from World Bank Funded Projects*: British Embassy, Washington 1991.
9 *Code of Ethics and Professional Conduct*: AIA, Washington 1991.
10 *Extortion and Bribery in Business Transactions*: ICC, Paris 1977.
11 *The White Book Guide*: FIDIC, Lausanne 1991.
12 *The Aid and Trade Provision – Guidelines for Applicants*: DTI/ODA, London 1988.
13 *Overseas Projects Fund – Guidance for Applicants*: DTI, London 1990.
14 *Revised Recommendations Concerning International Competitions in Architecture and Town Planning*: UNESCO, Paris 1978.
15 *International Competitions*: IUA, Paris 1988.
16 Architecture and Politics: *RIBA Journal*, **98** (6) 42, 43 (June 1991).
17 *Guidelines for Ad-hoc Collaboration Agreements between Consulting Firms*: FIDIC, Lausanne 1977.

18 *Standard Form of Agreement for the Appointment of an Architect*: RIBA Publications Ltd, London 1992.

19 *Plan of Work for Design Team Operations*: RIBA Publications Ltd, London 1988.

20 *Client/Consultant Model Services Agreement*: FIDIC, Lausanne 1990.

21 A Konya: *Design Primer for Hot Climates*: The Architectural Press, London 1980 (op).

22 Hassan Fathy: *Natural Energy and Vernacular Architecture*: University of Chicago Press 1986.

23 *Building Overseas in Warm Climates*: Building Research Establishment, Watford 1985.

24 *Overseas Building Notes*: Building Research Establishment, Watford 1991.
   OBN 196 on Health aspects of latrine construction (June 1991) lists 36 titles in print from 1972 onwards.

25 Evelyn Lip: *Chinese Geomancy*: Times Books International, Singapore 1979.

26 John Bennett: *International Construction Project Management*: Butterworth-Heinemann, Oxford 1991.

27 J Mole: *Mind Your Manners*: The Industrial Society, London 1990.

28 JoAnn Craig: *Culture Shock*: Times Books International, Singapore 1979.

29 W Somerset Maugham: *Malaysian Stories*: Heinemann Asia, Hong Kong 1978.

30 *Dictionary of Building Terms*: Moscow 1986 (available from the RIBA Bookshop).

31 Rene David and John E C Brierley: *Major Legal Systems in the World Today*: Stevens & Sons, London 1985.

32 Anthony Speight and Gregory Stone: *Architect's Legal Handbook*: Butterworth-Heinemann Ltd 1991.

33 G Golzen: *The Daily Telegraph Guide to Working Abroad*: Kogan Page, London 1992.

34 N R Mansfield: "Some international issues from the early 1989s facing British consulting engineers": *Proceedings of the Institution of Civil Engineers* Part I, **80**, 1211–1231 (October 1986).

Note: (op) indicates that a reference is out of print.

Index

Page numbers in **bold type** indicate a main reference.